The

Totalitarian State

Of America

Copyright©2020 by Germinal G. Van
All Rights Reserved
Book written by Germinal G. Van
Cover designed by Germinal G. Van
Published by Germinal G. Van and Kindle Direct Publishing
authorgerminalgvan@gmail.com
ISBN: 978-107-101-2901

Printed in the United States

GERMINAL G. VAN

THE
TOTALITARIAN STATE
OF AMERICA

A Critique of American Government

By the same Author

American Political Culture

Equal Under the Law

Essays On Issues (Volume 1)

Reflection On Identity Politics

The Efficiency of Capitalism

Democratic Socialism On Trial

The Problem Of Egalitarianism

Income Inequality and Economics

Market Economy and The State

Table of Contents

Foreword

Ask the average American what they love about their country and you will hear one common sentiment shared by many of them: they love America because America is free. "Freedom" is a word that has been, however, bastardized by many so that it can be used to manufacture consent amongst people who do not even give time to try to think or to understand the issues that surround them. America is no exception. Ever-growing politicians and talking heads who aim to push the status-quo of the ever-growing American state to bombard us with rhetoric about how great America is because of our

"Freedom." Many people buy into this, and because of their buying into it, they never bother to actually learn what freedom truly is.

To live under a surveillance state is not the same as living under a state of freedom. To live under a police state is not the same as living under a state of freedom. To live under a state of economic interventionism, which only fuels the fascist corporatist system and robs the common man, is not the same as living under a state of liberty where individuals are free from government coercion. America is all of these things, and thus, it is not a free country, and it has failed to be a free country for a very long time.

The part of the American state that has had the most negative impact on the United States, is the foreign policy that has made America not just the world's police because of their intervention in major wars (World War 1 & 2, Vietnam, wars in the Middle East etc.), their use of the CIA to reach political means (Angola, Chile, Nicaragua···etc.). It has caused blowback, which created terrorist groups who are a reactionary force against US imperialism around the world (Al Qaeda, the Contras, ISIS, Khmer Rouge, the Taliban, etc.) has led to an array of problems for the nation that is America. First of all, this terrible policy may have led to a good economy, but it was only beneficial for the state and the corporations that it subsidizes (corporations who often treat their employees badly and get away with it due to the state letting them bypass numerous forms of regulations and licensing). Second of all, this type of foreign policy makes America not only a current and historic evil empire, but a future one as well. The CIA blowback has proven that the enemies of our enemies will only become our enemies when we are their friends. Third, arguably and most importantly, it kills the moral of our nation. Inflation, which is, one way, caused by wars; received infinite support from the central bank (the Federal Reserve). This support from the Federal Reserve has been leading to constant boom-and-bust cycles in America. In these cases, only small businesses and the common man are hurt, while big business and the elite are subsidized, and therefore saved from serious trouble. Along with this, many veterans who came back become bitter with the state they have served, once they have realized how much they sacrificed and lost serving the coercive corporations of America that serve the political powers who I call the American Mafia. It is a shame that more American citizens are no more informed and outraged at how many honest, good people, both foreign and domestic, lose their lives because of these needless and endless wars.

Currently, and historically, the United States is a country that has been engaged in a war upon its own citizens. The War on Drugs, for example, has criminalized people's voluntary choices and created black markets which unleashed violence from gangs and enabled authoritarian policing on innocent people and on communities, who are usually low-income people and members of minority groups. Citizens like Ross Ulbricht, who created the famous website "The Silk Road," are serving life sentences over non-violent "crimes" while elitist sexual predators like Harvey Weinstein or former U.S. Senator Al Franken; are free and live privileged lives. The grossly titled "Patriot Act" is not patriotic by any means, but rather totalitarian. The fact that it is legal for bureaucrats to spy on regular American citizens makes it apparent that Americans are not free, but rather need to watch what they say and who they say it to. This is a fact, despite the first and fourth amendments of our precious constitution, which have been manipulated by bureaucrats so that it will favor the state rather than the citizens.

This is no accident, however. This horrific foreign policy, which matched with criminal domestic policy; is all part of the plots of zealots who we refer to as "democratically elected leaders." Soon after the Declaration of Independence was written, the Federalists began to treat it as though it was a mandate to create a central government. Then when the Constitution was drafted, approved and enacted, it was then seen as the mandate, by the state and its bureaucracy, which gave the government the right to intervene on a certain basis, rather than it being seen for what it is by the people: the mandate which restricts government in favor of the freedom of the people. The Constitution would then go on to be abused by presidents (in the name of vague terms such as "national security," "national interest," or "public policy"), so that they could use their power to expand the scope of the state, and make the centralized government even more powerful. This allowed for the government to force its interests and control into our daily lives more and more as history went on. Throughout history, it has been common for the state to take advantage of tragedies and emergencies, to legislate around, and make it seem as if government is not the cause of problems, however, that it is the only the solution to all of them. The Great Depression is no exception.

Often derailed as a failure of capitalism, the Great Depression was actually the fault of misguided economic policy along with government intervention into the banks and the creation of unbacked credit out of thin air. However, schools (which answer to the state's interest and control) have taught Americans differently. Instead of being taught the truth about history, we are taught that FDR was a hero, and his centrally-planned economy and his intrusive government policies that worked off the backs of the American people, are the epitome of American "Freedom." Ever since the time of FDR, the American Fascist Corporatist state has only become more totalitarian and has only become more overreaching in its quest for a new world order which would serve the states and elitists across the world, and which would trample on the common man and his inalienable rights to life and liberty.

Propaganda, which has served its many purposes for the state, has probably shined the most when you start to see that the state has coated the fascist war machine with the mask of patriotism and the reasons of "spreading democracy." Again, these bastardizations of words have led to the manufactured consent that has allowed for terrible things to happen at the helm of only the most powerful people in the United States, who many times are in partnership with those other corrupt statistics across the world. I emphasize upon this because I do believe that this means America's misfortunes could lead to actions from America and many other countries, both for and against it, that would mean very grim consequences for innocent people across the world.

This has all been made possible through the establishment of a central bank in America. The Federal Reserve; the entity that controls the money supply and interest rates, has been the fuel that has funded the flames that is the American war machine. At the same time, American citizens are losing value in their money and the economy is being artificially pushed in the wrong directions for those regular private citizens.

This all proves the common sentiment espoused by those against the state: if you give the state an inch, it will take a mile. Anarchists like myself, concede that under any type of state, freedom cannot exist. However, it is radical minarchists like Germinal G. Van who inspire me and get me to try and work with the political tools available to me, similar to the way Lew Rockwell is inspired by Ron Paul.

For instance, Germinal and myself agree that we should live in a free society. That means people should be able to choose what they want to do with themselves, as long as they are not initiating violence against other people, along with not stealing or damaging their property. For this to be possible, the society must be one that has a free market. I will allow Murray Rothbard to explain my assertion:

"Free-market capitalism is a network of free and voluntary exchanges in which producers work, produce, and exchange their products for the products of others through prices voluntarily arrived at. State capitalism consists of one or more groups making use of the coercive apparatus of the government — the State — to accumulate capital for themselves by expropriating the production of others by force and violence."

Murray N. Rothbard, *Capitalism versus Statism*

Under this free-market system, people will be free to make whatever choices they want to, and they can benefit off this both personally and economically as long as they adhere to the strict principle of non-aggression, which as, I have said before, means to not hurt people or arbitrarily deprive them of their property. Even voluntary socialism can take place, just do not include me in it, and we are fine.

Where Germinal and I disagree, obviously, and many people think it could play a dividing factor, is how we think this system should play out. Germinal is a classical liberal, and a libertarian minarchist. He believes that the state still has a role to play in society, but its role shall be restricted to its most elemental functions such as providing adjudication through the law, provide military and policing services. I am a free-market anarchist. I believe that the state should simply not exists because its mere existence would lead to the deprivation of individual liberty. I, and many anarcho-capitalists, believe that the law, the police and the military should be privatized in order to avoid state monopoly. The reason this does not play for a dividing factor for the both of us, is because we both logically agree on the fact that free-market capitalism has never been tried.

While being a free-market anarchist, I do admire the work of very few people that would be considered politicians. Ron Paul, for instance, is a hero of mine. And there are people who are making their runs at this time, who I believe will be great for the liberty movement. Men like Maj Touré, Joshua Smith, or Joshua Flynn.

I, myself, even run an umbrella libertarian student group which educates students and together performs voluntary community projects to show that "voluntaryism" can work. In that group, I work with classical liberals, and even, surprisingly, with some libertarian socialists, and mutualists. If people like that can exist, and be as consistent as they have, along with groups of people being so inspired by the message that they decide to actually carry out in their lives and work together in the pursuit of their own self-interests, why not work together to try and get the most free market system we could possibly get?

As for Germinal himself, I think very highly of this man. He is the author of nine books and contributes to writing articles to the amazing *Mises Institute*, which educates children and the average citizen in the field of Austrian economics, along with contributing to the *Libertarian Institute* and the *Foundation for*

Economic Freedom (FEE). He is also the Fundraising Chair of the Libertarian Party of Chicago, and a political advisor to Libertarian State House for Illinois 78th district candidate Joshua Flynn.

However, I still believe Germinal is selling himself short, or at least, does not understand what he is working towards. Writers like Germinal G. Van are so few and far between. When I think of how prolific and convincing, he is; I am reminded of writers like Rothbard or Rockwell, with his writings on economics and society. Let us not forget how amazing and convincing he is in the philosophy department as well. Germinal G. Van is a leader, and his name will be one highly spoken of in due time.

As an anarchist, I am more than excited to be a part of this work where my good friend will do his part in exposing the state for what it is.

As someone who loves to learn, I am curious to see how he will show how this can be done by preserving the most absolute minarchist state.

I would like to speak for both Germinal and I, by leaving with those quote that should live within the hearts of all of those who fight for liberty:

"Tu ne cede malis, sed contra audentior ito – Do not give into evil but proceed ever so boldly against it."

Ludwig Von Mises

Keep on fighting the good fight, Germinal.

Stratton J. Davis,
November 11, 2019

About the Author

Germinal G. Van is an author, political essayist, libertarian scholar, public speaker, and political philosopher. He is the Former Fundraising Chair of the Libertarian Party of Chicago, a political advisor to the campaign of Libertarian candidate for Illinois State House, Joshua Flynn; and a member of the Midwest Political Science Association. Mr. Van has published several books including *Reflection On Identity Politics, The Problem Of Egalitarianism,* and *Income Inequality and Economics.* Mr. Van has also published several articles with the *Mises Institute,* the *Libertarian Institute* and the

Foundation for Economic Education (FEE). Mr. Van holds a bachelor's degree in political science from the Catholic University of America and a master's degree from the George Washington University. The writings of Mr. Van mainly focus on political philosophy, political economy, and social theory. *The Totalitarian State Of America* is Mr. Van's tenth book.

Acknowledgements

The completion of this book occurred mainly thanks to three people who have dearly contributed. First, my wife. As usual, she has been an essential support to all the books I have published.

Second, I would like thank Joshua Flynn for always contributing to the intellectual output of this book. His contribute has been ever since preponderant for the development of new ideas.

Lastly, I would like to thank my friend Stratton J. Davis, a dedicated activist and intellectual devoted to the cause of liberty. Stratton has significantly contributed to the completion of this manuscript with a perspicuous foreword. I am looking forward to collaborating with him for my forthcoming works.

Preface

Totalitarianism, in its strict sense and most narrowed definition, is the absolute of coercion. Coercion is, not necessarily nor primarily, the use of physical force. Coercion is the use of various means that seeks to compel someone to do something that he or she did not intend to do voluntarily. For example, persuasion is a form of coercion because the one who persuades, also known as the persuader; imposes in a way; his will power on the one who lets himself being persuaded. He, therefore, forces the persuaded one to change his mind and to perform an action that the persuaded did not initially think of. The subsequent action performed by the persuaded is not an action grounded on free will because his or her decision to perform that action was coerced by an external factor. This factor is the element exerting the coercion upon the one executing that initially unwilling action. Thus, coercion is anything that forces someone to do something that he or she did not intend to do it willingly or freely, including physical force. Consequently, taxation is a form of coercion imposed on people. Coercive physical force such as imprisonment may be used against the individual who fails to pay his taxes.

Today, I believe that we do live in a totalitarian state. The United States is considered to be a free country. It is even called "the land of the free." But how can we be the land of the free if the people cannot even choose the tax system that they believe could be best for society? How can we be the land of the free when the state decides, without the consent of the governed, the rate at which people should be taxed? How can we be the land of the free when nine judges have decided, without consulting the consent of the governed, that abortion is a legal right? How can we be the land of the free and a nation of laws when bureaucrats are not held accountable before the law for implementing the wrong policies that hurt thousands and millions of ordinary citizens? How can we be the land of the free when the state decides under what price system labor should be supplied? How can we be the land of the free when law enforcement officers, on a daily basis, infringe upon the most elemental rights of the individual living a free society, including fatally shooting unarmed citizens? How can we be the land of the free when the government spies on citizens and attempts to control their narrative and thoughts? All these rhetorical questions point to the fact that our society is definitely not free. Our society is completely subjected to a totalitarianism enforced by the federal government of the United States. A totalitarianism in which the legal rules and regulations are used as tools to control to the greatest extent possible, the behavior of the citizens like Big Brother controlled the behavior of his citizens in *1984.*

I chose to write this book in order to denounce the current system in which we live in. The United States is no longer the land of the free. It is a totalitarian state in which the United States government is a gigantic organization that uses a system of coercion to ascertain civil policy. I chose to write this book because I believe that the ordinary citizen shall be aware that he does no longer live in a free society where his most elemental rights are constantly violated and undermined by a government that only cares about expanding its own authority over our lives.

My objective, through writing this book, is to stimulate the reader and the ordinary citizen, to begin claiming for the federal government to be limited, and to make him understand that our Constitution has been undermined by a totalitarian state whereby politicians and bureaucrats only care about their own power and prestige than serving the people who have entrusted them.

Germinal G. Van
March 2019

Introduction

When the Founding Fathers debated on the
Articles and Amendments that would be
configurated in the Constitution of the United
States, they were all, nonetheless, in agreement,
including Alexander Hamilton with reluctance;
that it was imperative to ensure that the United
States does never become a tyranny. To achieve
this, of course, the Framers of the Constitution
have decided to design a government that would
be strong enough to preserve the rights and
freedoms of its citizens, but not excessively
mighty to enslave them. This is how James

Madison, John Jay, Alexander Hamilton, Thomas Jefferson, George Washington, George Mason, Benjamin Franklin, and many other prominent American thinkers; have generated a government with few and defined enumerated powers only proposed and bounded by law. Thus, the concept of limited government has been enacted into law in 1789.

The political philosophy of the American republic was unequivocally based on the principles of classical liberalism; which means economic freedom, individual liberties, the right to private property, and the rule of law. The American republic has never been conceived with the aim of giving more power to the federal government, but on the contrary, to limit as much as possible its authority which, eventually and unavoidably, becomes a predatory authority if unchecked. The Founding Fathers chose for

America, classical liberalism over any other political philosophy because they understood that the highest aim of individuals is the pursuit of happiness. The pursuit of happiness means having the freedom for oneself to pursue his own interests. And it is this philosophy for which they wanted to make it the motto of the republic.

244 years after the Declaration of Independence, America has changed. Evidently, the world is changing, and nothing can remain stationary, but America has changed for the worst over the years. Physical and material changes are surely customary mechanisms of the world's evolution, but the spirit and mindset that determine the fundamentals of a society cannot change because it is what ascertains its cultural identity. The spirit of the United States today is no longer the same as the one that the Founding Fathers have bequeathed us. The

American people have become intrinsically dependent on the good graces of the federal government. Many Americans see the federal government as the new God; as the new messiah that will bring salvation to his people. The federal government we have today is no longer the one that James Madison has envisioned. The federal government that we currently have is a government that has violated the scope of its most elemental constitutional prerogatives. We now have an omniscient and omnipotent government; alas, inordinately commanding and authoritative that needs to be contained as a dangerous dog in a cage that has not bitten yet but will if it has the opportunity to harm. The current government we have, is a disproportionately mighty and a totalitarian government. Totalitarian; because it is involved in all aspects of the citizens' life and controls our decision-making. The federal government, although it does not, yet, retain the monopoly of the means of production, nevertheless, controls the economy because it controls the value of money as well as it enforces regulations which attenuate competition between businesses and incentivize an increased crony capitalism. The government also controls industries such as education, or urban housing; and effectuates means-tested programs to keep those at the bottom of social norms, in a perpetual state of poverty. It also commands a substantial part of our healthcare system, which every year, increases the cost of healthcare in the United States. The federal government now controls language through political correctness and unjustly and unlawfully punishes those who would abridge the new linguistic system that it is subtly implementing. The federal government ruthlessly rules over individuals through the manipulation of emotions, language, and the collective brainwashing of politicians over the uneducated; to expand its power, which gradually becomes absolute.

The infelicitous and obvious veracity that we must face today is that classical liberalism is literally on the precipice. The classical liberalism of this new era is not the one that James Madison or Thomas Jefferson wanted to bequeath us. Things must be said as they are; classical liberalism is slowly and progressively dying in America. It has already died in Europe after World War II except in Great Britain when it was revived during the premiership of Mrs. Thatcher under the guise of neoliberalism. In America, classical liberalism has converged towards social liberalism; a liberalism in which freedom is conditional, restrictive and arbitrarily determined by the authority of the state. It is that liberalism used in Continental Europe. The America we have today is an America that would please John Rawls's egalitarian vision of society; however, it would authenticate the concerns that Hayek had raised in *The Road to Serfdom.*

The Totalitarian State of America: A Critique of American Government is a collection of political essays whose central purpose is to denounce the exponential proliferation of the powers of the federal government towards a more consolidated totalitarianism. I am not an anarcho-capitalist. I do not believe in anarchy. I am not calling for the dissolution of the federal government. What I do advocate for, is a return to the nineteenth-century liberalism; a liberalism in which economic freedom, and individual rights were at the center of society's core values. I am advocating for a society in which government is limited and strictly reduced to its initial constitutional scope as the Founding Fathers have foreseen.

This book is also an uncompromising defense of classical liberalism as the true liberalism that must be reinstated as the first value that defines the United States of America. The book is composed of ten distinctive essays. The first essay stresses the woes of the welfare state. It decries the pernicious welfare policies that the government enacts in order to alleviate poverty. The second essay evaluates the mechanism whereby the government exerts a significant influence on employment as well as social protection programs. This essay argues that the labor laws imposed by government make it difficult for employers to hire or fire as well as it criticizes that the insertion of social protection payment is a coercive government method that requires the employee to have a substantial portion of his paycheck withdrawn, which leaves him with not much to spend. The employee could use that money to pay for his own protection rather than letting the government providing him that protection that costs more than it actually worth. The third essay articulates on the magnitude and considerable ascendance that the government exercises on the populations that are uneducated about the healthcare system. By making believing a major part of the national population that, access to healthcare is a fundamental right; the government positions itself as the guarantor of that right, which means that it is the one that retains authority over medical supply. The fourth essay is a severe criticism of the progressive income taxation. It explicates that the use of the progressive income taxation allows the federal government to tax the wealthy at a higher rate so that it could invest in its programs. Yet these programs have produced outcomes that do not promulgate the advancement of those who are in the low-income threshold. The fifth essay is relatively self-explanatory. Political correctness is the tool that the government has been using to control the mainstream narrative. To control the mainstream narrative is the centerpiece for government to establish its totalitarian power over the people and to control their mind. The sixth essay is a critique of the method by which the government is determined to influence the economy at all costs. However, fiscal policy, which is also known as tax policy, stimulates more inflation, which devalues the value of money. The seventh essay is centralized upon social justice. It argues that social justice is merely a pretext for the federal government to meddle in social affairs, which is a domain strictly reserved to individuals and not to a central authority to interfere. The eighth essay aims to demonstrate how the police has become militarized. Police officers have gradually become machines that do not hesitate to use excessive force to impose its law rather than using more conventional and less coercive methods to ensure law and order. The ninth essay criticizes the Supreme Court. In fact, the Justices of the Supreme Court no longer interpret the Constitution in its original intent, but rather interpret it in a sense that gives them the power to legislate their ideas from the bench so that they become law. The tenth and last essay of this manuscript deals with the fact that too much government encroachment in economic and social affairs leads inevitably to central planning. However, the market is the best and the most suitable place to ensure that the allocation of resources is adequately redistributed rather than letting the government being in charge of everything and mismanaging resources.

1.

The Welfare State:
The Surest Way To Maintain
Inequality

The welfare state in the United States was created in the 1930s as a response to the Great Depression. It was generated with the best of intentions but did not produce the outcome that everyone has expected. A sure result that the welfare state has generated though, is the expansion and the amplification of the federal government's powers which went far beyond its constitutional scope. When the Great Depression began, about 18 million elderly, disabled, and single mothers with children already lived at a bare subsistence level in the United States.[1] State and local governments together with private charities helped these people.[2] By 1933, another 13 million Americans had been thrown out of work—suddenly, state and local governments and charities could no longer provide even minimum assistance for all those in need.[3]

A federal welfare system was a radical break from the past.[4] Americans had always prided themselves on having a strong sense of individualism and self-reliance.[5] The effects of the Great Depression were so economically and

---

[1] Editors, "BRIA 14 3 How Welfare Began in the United States," *Bill of Rights in Action,* Constitutional Rights Foundation. (1998). Article.

[2] Ibid.
[3] Ibid.
[4] Ibid.
[5] Ibid.

socially damaging that the federal government had no choice but to intervene. This intervention was, however, a boon for President Roosevelt because it allowed him to expand the prerogatives of the federal government far beyond its constitutionally limited powers. The emphasis during the first two years of President Franklin Roosevelt's "New Deal" was to provide work relief for the millions of unemployed Americans.[6] In his State of the Union Address before Congress on January 4, 1935, President Roosevelt declared: "The time has come for action by the national government to provide security against the major hazards and vicissitudes of life."[7] He went on to propose the creation of federal unemployment and old-age insurance programs.[8] By permanently expanding

---

[6] Ibid.
[7] Ibid.
[8] Ibid.

federal responsibility for security for all Americans, Roosevelt believed that the necessity for government make-work employment and other forms of Depression relief would disappear.[9] Roosevelt's intentions were certainly arguably noble on the moral aspect. On the political aspect nonetheless, the essence of his intentions actually authenticated the social contract theory of Hobbes. Roosevelt was, in fact, the leviathan that Hobbes described in his work. All those who benefited from the New Deal programs, in reality, have capitulated their rights to the sovereign in exchange for obtaining economic and social security. Roosevelt himself, was not the sovereign per se; the real sovereign was the federal government, and the welfare state was the social contract that established the covenant between the

---

[9] Ibid.

subject (rather than citizen) and the sovereign. Recipients of welfare programs were no longer masters of their own political, economic and social destiny because their freedom was conditioned by the policies that the federal government implemented in these programs in order to acquire more participants. The root of this new social contract which is the welfare state; has indeed incentivized a climate of social dependence vis-à-vis the government, and the relinquishment of the personal responsibility of the individual.

"The road to hell is paved with good intentions." This ancient proverb which originated from Saint Bernard of Clairvaux, is a pure validation of what the policies of the New Deal were. The New Deal aimed, in theory, to alleviate and mitigate the level of poverty in order to have more equality. However, the New

Deal in particular; and welfare state policies in general; have created more inequality. New Deal programs were financed by tripling federal taxes from $1.6 billion in 1933 to 5.3 billion in 1940.[10] The most important sources of New Deal revenues were excise taxes levied on alcoholic beverage, cigarettes, matches, candy, chewing gum, margarine, fruit juice, soft drinks, cars, tires, telephone calls, movie tickets, playing cards, electricity, radios—these and many other everyday things were subject to New Deal excise taxes, which meant that the New Deal was substantially financed by the middle-class and the poor.[11] Until 1937, New Deal revenue from excise taxes exceeded the combined revenue from both personal income taxes and

---

[10] Powell, Jim, *How FDR's New Deal Harmed Millions of Poor People*. Cato Institute. (2003). Article. Web.

[11]Ibid.

corporate income taxes.[12] It was not until 1942, in the midst of World War II, that income taxes exceeded excise taxes for the first time under FDR—consumers had less money to spend, and employers had less money for growth and jobs.[13] Furthermore, New Deal taxes destroyed jobs in 1930s, which prolonged unemployment that averaged 17 percent.[14] Higher business taxes meant that employers had less money for growth and jobs.[15] The National Industrial Recovery Act of 1933 cut back production and forced wages above market levels, making it more expensive for employers to hire people—blacks alone were estimated to have lost some 500,000 jobs because of that same policy.[16] The New Deal failed because Roosevelt misunderstood what

---

[12] Ibid.
[13] Ibid.
[14] Ibid.
[15] Ibid.
[16] Ibid.

caused the Great Depression.[17] He failed to understand that the Great Depression occurred due to a shortage of money supply from the Federal Reserve to commercial banks, which dropped the interest rates to 30 percent and created a deflation. That deflation subsequently generated the stock market crash of 1929. It was certainly not a failure of the free-market and laissez-faire economics. The federal government, by stifling competition and efficiency, failed to recognize that price cuts are in the benefit of the consumer because price cuts lead to cheaper and better food.[18] The government reduced competition by adjusting commodity prices for inflation and parity from a period when farm prices were high. As a result,

---

[17] Daniel, *Why Did The New Deal Fail?* Medium.com. (2016). Article. Web.

[18] Ibid.

prices of food increased in the 1930s[19] which made it very hard for those unemployed at that time to actually purchase food as they please. It is undeniable that the Great Depression has allowed Roosevelt, and the subsequent politicians in favor of statism, to expand the federal government. Therefore, as stated; the federal government has become this permanent entity involved in economic and social affairs. The New Deal was the very first batch of policies that engaged the federal government toward a precarious totalitarianism.

The 1960s were the period when the federal government has reached its peak. It was the time when the federal government became unavoidable, ubiquitous, and omnipotent. And the individual who has managed to give this oversized power to the federal government, was

---

[19] Ibid.

no other than President Lyndon Baines Johnson (LBJ). When Lyndon B. Johnson was elected President of the United States in 1964, he wanted to fundamentally transform American society as Barack Obama wanted to do so forty-five years later. This fundamental transformation that took place under LBJ's leadership had one major objective: that the ordinary American citizen relies on the federal government to alleviate his problems. In other words, this transformation was to kill individualism and to give place to collectivism; to replace classical liberalism with social liberalism, and to substitute liberty for equality; because the quest for equality is what enables government to be in charge of arbitrarily decide what is right from what is wrong. Once president, Johnson has passed a series of policies such as Medicare and Medicaid, which empowered the federal government to have a permanent foothold in the healthcare industry; the Primary and Secondary Education Act, which warranted the federal government to subsidize schools and to administer a national curriculum; and Affirmative Action policies, which enhances the capacity of the federal government to dictate schools the amount of students that they shall accept in order to receive public funds for research. There are many more legislations that President Johnson has invigorated by executive orders, but these one just mentioned were the most preeminent and were approved by Congress. It is important to fathom that President Johnson has, indeed, strengthened the authority of the central government in a totalitarian state.

The totalitarianism being discussed here, is not the brutal totalitarianism of the Soviet

Union, the communist states or even Nazi Germany. It is a tacit totalitarianism that seeks to enforce obedience through legal means. This form of totalitarianism could be perceived as a legal or soft totalitarianism because the government utilizes regulations to constrain economic freedom and to confiscate private property. Each law that is voted, or imposed by executive order, is a program that the federal government executes on society by mandatory taxation. The problem is that the government mismanages the programs that it is in charge of, which subsequently enlarges the inequality gap because those who are recipients of these programs remain economically stagnated. The U.S. Census Bureau has released its annual report for the year 2013 asserting that 14.5

percent of Americans were poor.[20] This percentage is almost the same exact rate as it was in 1967; three years after the War on Poverty started.[21] The welfare state imposed by President Johnson discouraged work and penalized marriages.[22] When the War on Poverty began, 7 percent of American children were born outside marriage.[23] Today, the number is 41 percent.[24] The welfare state is self-perpetuating. By undermining the social norms necessary for self-reliance, the welfare state creates a need for even greater assistance in the future.[25]

---

[20] Rector, Robert, *The War on Poverty: 50 years of Failure.* The Heritage Foundation. (2014). Article. Web.

[21] Ibid.
[22] Ibid.
[23] Ibid.
[24] Ibid.
[25] Ibid.

The term "welfare state" does not begin to encompass the totality of America's commitment of resources to aid the poor—it is more like a vast empire bigger than the entire budgets of almost every other country in the world.[26] America's welfare empire encompasses close to 200 or more federal and state programs, including 23 low-income health programs, 27 low-income housing programs, 30 employment and training programs, 34 social services programs, at least 13 food and nutrition programs, and 24 low-income child care programs.[27] With so many social programs available to the poor, how can we hope that the poor will be economically empowered to achieve self-sufficiency? The sad reality is that these

---

[26] Ferrera, Peter, *'Welfare State' Doesn't Adequately Describe How Much America's Poor Control Your Wallet.* Forbes. (2013). Article. Web.

[27] Ibid.

means-tested programs are a way for the federal government to keep the poor poorer and as its loyal voters because the welfare recipients will continue to vote in favor of the political party or for a candidate that aims to expand these means-tested programs. The welfare recipient does not want to lose his privilege of receiving benefits for which he does not work for so he will keep supporting government welfare policies so long as it benefits him. This is how the totalitarian state works. No one is free under its control. We all become slaves and we are subjugated to its predatory power. With the welfare state in place, income inequality is sure to prevail so the poor will keep electing politicians that will enforce welfare policies in exchange for votes.

2.

Unemployment
and
Social Protection

There are several factors that lead to the rise of unemployment such as the minimum wage law, economic recession, punitive labor laws against employers and business owners, and many other factors. In this essay, my sole and genuine intention is to focus on one aspect that creates an augmentation of unemployment; which is, of course, the minimum wage law. In addition to demonstrating that the minimum wage law is arguably pernicious especially to the low-skilled workers and employment-seekers; I also endeavor to substantiate that social protection is also a predicament for the wage-earner because it is compulsorily associated with the employee's paycheck and subsequently deducted from his remuneration without true consent.

The Fair Labor Standard Act of 1938, also known as the minimum wage law, was implemented by the federal government in 1938. The law stated that an employer could not pay an employee no less than $0.25 an hour. The minimum wage has never remained a stationary remuneration. It increases every year by a couple cents or sometimes a dollar unit. During the first decade following its enactment, the minimum wage law did not yet affect low-skilled employees and job seekers adversely because inflation was relatively high; so, employers could pay employees at wages well above the minimum wage. Inflation from 1940 to 1949 was on average 5.52 percent per year, consequently, the total cumulative inflation for the entire decade was 69.78 percent.[28] It is, however, imperative to comprehend the essence of the minimum wage law. It is essentially a discriminatory legislation because the government compels the employer to openly discriminate against low-skilled individuals.

It is a conundrum because the federal government interferes in a voluntary and mutual contract between the employer and the employee. When the employer hires a job-seeker and the job-seeker accepts the terms and conditions that the employer offers him; a voluntary and mutual agreement takes place between the employer and the employee. The

---

[28] *Inflation and CPI Consumer Index 1940-1949*, InflationData.com. (2019). Index Charts.

employee agrees to work for a salary that the employer considers appropriate and adequate to the skills of the employee who just got hired, especially if that employee has never been hired beforehand or has never acquired sufficient professional experience in the workplace. The absence of the minimum wage law would enable the voluntary transaction between the employer and the employee to take place because the employee is gaining work experience, developing a new skill and financially meeting ends need. The employer, on the other hand, was using the skills of the employee to develop the production of the company. Without the minimum wage law, an employer could hire who he wants according to the needs and goals of the company. This allowed many youngsters without prior professional work experience to have a job and to be lifted out of poverty. The minimum wage law imposed by the federal government hinders low-skilled individuals from being employed because no employer would want to take the risk of hiring an individual whose skills are well below the skills that the job requires for its completion. Employers do not want to spend money on resources to train a low-skilled worker who has no experience and pay him more than what he truly worth. So, the employer is forced to discriminate against the low-skilled worker and must hire someone who has previous work experience in the industry and pay him higher wages due to his previous work experience. Thus, many low-skilled workers remain unemployed.

Minimum wage increases, which intended to boost pay for low-income workers, ended up increasing unemployment according to a new study conducted by Professor Jeffrey Clemens and published by the National Bureau of Economic Research.[29] The study found that minimum wage increases reduced employment opportunities for low-skilled workers by nearly six points during the Great Recession of 2008.[30] Between December 2006 and December 2009, employment among individuals ages 16 to 30 with less than a high school degree declined from 40 percent to 28 percent.[31] It is an undeniable fact that every time that the federal government increases the minimum wage, unemployment significantly grows. The current

---

[29] McMorris, Bill, *Wage Hikes Depressed Low-Skilled Unemployment.* The Washington Free Beacon. (2016). Article. Web.

[30] Ibid.

[31] Clemens, Jeffrey, *The Minimum Wage and The Great Recession: Evidence from The Current Population Survey.* National Bureau of Economic Research. (2015). Article.

federal minimum wage was set at $7.25 an hour in 2009.

Politicians like Bernie Sanders, Alexandria Ocasio-Cortez, Kamala Harris, Kirsten Gillibrand and many more left-wing political leaders, are pushing for the minimum wage to be set at $15-an-hour because they believe that raising the minimum wage to $15-an-hour will make living wage for low-skilled workers. These politicians do either not understand economics, or they are knowingly ignoring the facts simply because they are stimulated by maintaining more power over an arguably uneducated populace, which means; including raising the minimum wage if necessary, to retain control over unemployment. The myth that has been persisting for years is that politicians tell ordinary citizens who do not understand much about the mechanism of economics; that the minimum wage is the most predictable indicator that leads to a living wage. That the more we increase the minimum wage, the closer we get to a living wage standard. Whereas the living wage is absolutely not based on the minimum wage but only on the market value. Living wage is based upon the market value, and the market value is based on inflation because the rate of inflation is what determines prices of goods and services on the market. If inflation is low, more workers could reach living wage standard easily because what they earn would be sufficient enough to meet ends need since prices are relatively low. For example, a worker that earns $13 an hour can easily make living wage if he lives in Kentucky or rural Texas because the market value in these areas is relatively low. If that same worker who earns $14 an hour lives in Washington, D.C., he is, therefore, below living wage because the minimum wage in Washington, D.C. is $14 an hour. The market value in Washington, D.C. is significantly higher than the one in Texas or Kentucky. An increase to $15 an hour will have a larger adversarial effect on workers earning much less than $15 than it will on workers earning closer to $15 when the wage increase goes into effect.[32] The restaurant industry, for example, is the most affected by such augmentation because it is the industry where most workers are wage-earners and paid by the hour. A $1 increase in the minimum wage leads to a 14 percent increase the likelihood of exit the typical mid-size restaurant,[33] which means a

---

[32] Millsap, Adam, *How Higher Minimum Wages Impact Employment,* Forbes. (2018). Article. Web.

[33] Dara Lee Luca and Michael Luca, *Survival of the Fittest: The Impact of the minimum Wage on Firm Exit.* Harvard Business

mid-size restaurant (3.5 star) is on the brink to go out of business. When the minimum wage increases, businesses are required, not by law, but by economic common sense, to raise their prices in order to stay in business otherwise they will be drawn out by the unjust competition. Raising prices of goods and services forces businesses to hire less which in turn makes many low-skilled unemployed.

Now the great question here is to know then why the federal government continues to raise the minimum wage knowing that this increase penalizes low-skilled workers and incentivizes more unemployment? For the simple reason that the minimum wage law enables the federal government to have the

School, Mathematica Policy Research. (2017-2018). Working Paper 17-088. Article.

monopoly over the labor market as any totalitarian government would do in order to control economic output. Economic regulations empower the federal government to regulate competition, which gives corporations a competitive advantage over startups and mid-sized businesses. Bureaucrats in Washington know for a fact that corporations such as Big Techs or General Motors, can easily overcome the constraints of the augmentation of the minimum wage. An advantage that startups and mid-sized businesses do not have and will not have so long as the federal government is the one that determines wages for the market.

There is indeed a reason why wage-earners, that is to say those who constitute the middle-class and the working-class; cannot effortlessly increase their wealth. This reason is obviously social protection. What social protection is? Social protection is any public and private benefit program dedicated to the protection of the worker such as private health insurance, Social Security, Medicare, Medicaid, and many other programs compulsorily included by the federal government or by the employer as a deductible in the wage-earner's paycheck. Today, many jobs that once provided workers with economic security; have been replaced by temporary, part-time, and other contingent employment arrangements that offer few benefits or basic labor protections.[34] These typically low-paying and low-quality jobs are often the only ones available to low-income

---

[34] Gehr, Jessica, "Doubling Down: How Work Requirements in Public Benefit Programs Hurt Low-Wage Workers." *Policy Brief.* CLASP: Policy solutions that work for low-income people. (2017). Article.

individuals, meaning many workers are not able to earn enough to cover basic needs.[35]

Wage-earners unconsciously believed that when they receive their salary biweekly or monthly; that the employer is the one who pays for their social protection and that deduction of their paycheck was to merely repay the employer. It is, however, not the case. This misleadingly called the "employer's contribution" though it is in fact part of the employee's wage compulsorily deducted rather than paid out to him.[36] Imagine that instead of transferring money (the money deducted after the gross pay), the government offered employees a basket of "social protection"— insurance against illness, unemployment, or

[35] Ibid.
[36] Jasay, Anthony, "Paternalism and Employment," *Political Economy Concisely: Essays On Policy That Do Not Work and Markets That Do.* (2009). p.182. ISBN: 978-0-86597-778-5. Print.

destitution in old age.[37] If we make the assumption that collecting the tax and distributing it in the form of social protection are costless, the effect on the demand and supply of labor would depend on the difference between the cost of the package and the value attached to it by recipients.[38] At first sight, it would appear that employees would attach great value to social protection: reaction to proposals for curtailing benefits is usually virulent; but that is because most wage-earners are under the illusion that the greater part of the 'insurance premium' is being paid by someone other than themselves.[39] The point is 'social protection' costs more than it is worth to at least some of those that it protects.[40] In the meantime,

---

[37] Jasay, Anthony, *The Vicious Circle of Social Kindness,* Financial Times, (1994). Columns
[38] Ibid.
[39] Ibid.
[40] Ibid.

compulsory social insurance keeps the cash cost of labor way above the supply price of labor that would obtain if the wage paid in cash rather kind.[41] The fundamental cause about the cost of social protection is that, providing universal and mandatory social protection costs more than it is subjectively worth to the beneficiaries.[42] With all the additional costs of social protection that are imposed upon employees; it is unsurprisingly logical for wage-earners to have a hard time living beyond and above their means.

Government-mandated minimum wages, government-mandated and private social protections; are short-term gains that do create more unemployment and preclude the worker's

[41] Jasay, Anthony, "Paternalism and Employment," *Political Economy Concisely: Essays On Policy That Do Not Work and Markets That Do.* (2009). p.183. ISBN: 978-0-86597-778-5. Print.

[42] Ibid. p. 201.

ascension to a higher social class in the long-run. It is realistically and economically impossible for a low-skilled worker to begin making a living wage when bureaucrats augment the minimum wage, although the enactment of the minimum wage was designed specifically for them [low-skilled workers]. It is only in fairy-tale stories that the perfect scenario with the perfect actors would deliver an immaculate outcome. It is only in an immaterial world that the increased of the minimum wage would; in no way, shape or form; affect the cost of the market value. It is only in a surreal world that one can imagine that the minimum wage can increase, and the market value would remain motionless. Notwithstanding, the world in which we live in, offers us a much cold-hearted reality. Whenever the government increases the minimum wage, the prices of goods and services, as well as all the valuable assets that make up the value of the market such as the price of rent and property; increase concurrently. The market value is never stationary. It oscillates permanently. Since the surge of the minimum wage generates an increase of the market value; the surge of the market value, however, adversely reduces the purchasing power of the consumer in general and that of the low-skilled worker in particular. A high market value simultaneously increases the living wage. Therefore, a low-skilled worker cannot afford making a living wage if the government boosts the minimum wage every year. It is like climbing a mountain and expecting to reach its top, but this mountain is, in fact, a mountain without a peak for which its escalade is perpetual and in vain.

3.

Healthcare on Its Way to Becoming A "Right"

Many left-wing politicians, especially those on the progressive wing of the Democratic Party such as U.S. Senator Bernie Sanders, U.S. Senator Elizabeth Warren, U.S. Congresswoman Alexandria Ocasio-Cortez, U.S. Senator Kamala Harris, Former Tallahassee Mayor Andrew Gillum, Former Georgia State Representative Stacey Abrams, or Mayor Peter Buttigieg; have avowed that healthcare is a fundamental right that every single American citizen, regardless of his or her background; is and shall be entitled to. President Barack Obama has reiterated that same idea when he was the ruler of this nation and wanted to fundamentally change America for the better by taking it to the far-left.

Each of these politicians, except for President Obama, had indicated that healthcare is a fundamental right that every American must have access to, and this access must be subsidized by the federal government as a single-payer system. For the ordinary citizen who does not understand much about the functioning of the healthcare system, the right to healthcare seems a logically and justifiably reasonable cause that worth fighting for. Indeed, in a poll conducted by *Reuters* in 2018, 70 percent of Americans supported the proposal of a single-payer system.[43] This percentage shows how important healthcare is to Americans who spend a substantial portion of their paycheck on medical premiums and drug prescriptions. However, the ordinary citizen is unaware of the economic and social implications that it would entail if the healthcare system was strictly and solely managed by the bureaucrats of Washington who have obviously no clue about the medical condition of the average American citizen and the hardship that he or she is going through on a daily basis. The chief objective of this essay is to explicate to the ordinary and rational citizen, that healthcare is not a right per se and that a government-mandated healthcare system is not the adequate solution to attenuate

---

[43] Letitia Stein, Susan Cornwell, Joseph Tanfani, *Inside the Progressive Movement Roiling the Democratic Party.* Reuters. (2018). Article. Web.

the cost of healthcare nor to provide quality service to the national population.

During his inaugural address in 2009, President Obama has insisted that he was going to fundamentally transform American society. A key factor in this fundamental change was to subtly nationalize the healthcare system. President Obama may have not openly declared himself a socialist, but the platform on which he ruled for eight years was a platform on the borderline between social democracy and socialism. Either way, both ideologies advocated for a strong state intervention and government control over the means of production. The nationalization of the medical industry was a paramount objective to be achieved for the Obama administration, and a personal challenge for President Obama to be won. Roosevelt, Truman, JFK, LBJ, Jimmy Carter, and Bill Clinton have all failed in their quest to nationalize the medical industry. President Obama is the only president who has successfully yet partially nationalized the healthcare system of the United States. In 2010, President Obama has triumphantly but with strong opposition from Republicans and market-based lawmakers; legislated, with the help of the Supreme Court; the Affordable Care Act, also known as Obamacare. The implementation of Obamacare was a flexible and tacit nationalization of the medical industry.

When President Obama explained to the American people during the 2008 campaign his healthcare plan if he were president, and how he would operate it; he contended that those who are medically insured by a private insurance company could always keep their insurance premiums. Yet the effectuation of his healthcare program was drastically the opposite of his rhetoric on the issue. Once Obamacare became law of the land, the government would arbitrarily fine those who were medically insured by their private insurance company. The individual mandate and its enforcement fines were the "stick" behind the law.[44] Tax penalties for lack of coverage began accruing in 2014, and they were to phase in over a three-year period.[45] Taxpayers are penalized for lacking coverage for themselves and their dependents.[46] The purpose of Obamacare was to ensure that all Americans have at least the basic health coverage of the government's premium plan on top of their private insurance. This individual

---

[44] Associate Press. *Obamacare's Fines Are Not The Big Stick Everybody Thought,* Modern Healthcare. (2018). Article. Web.

[45] *What Is the Individual Mandate for Health Care Reform?* TurboTax. Updated in 2018. Article. Web.

[46] Ibid.

mandate, in spite of everything, imposed by the federal government, accurately demonstrates how President Obama has utilized legal coercive means to compel individuals to adopt his healthcare plan like a conventional totalitarian political regime would compel its citizens to forcefully approve a policy that they do not necessarily agree with. Overall, Obamacare was a disaster. All that program has done was to expand Medicaid. As a matter of fact, Obamacare failed to reform private insurance market.[47] If anything, it exacerbated the problems.[48] Obamacare's mandates and regulations forced premiums in the individual insurance market through the roof, pricing many middle-class families out of the insurance

---

[47] Editorials, *Obamacare Failure: Uninsured Rate Hasn't Budged In 3 years, CDC Says.* Investor's Business Daily. (2018). Article. Web.

[48] Ibid.

market all together.[49] One of the fundamental loopholes with the Affordable Care Act is that it was an ineffective healthcare program, like every program ran by a central authority. Although the bill was touted as a means to both cover the uninsured and help reduce costs for everyone,[50] the individual-mandate forces Americans to buy increasingly unaffordable health insurance or pay a tax.[51] With insurance premiums increasing at such a rapid rate, many in the middle-class are faced with higher and higher bills when visiting their doctor or a hospital.[52]

---

[49] Ibid.

[50] Hawkins, Marcus, *10 Reasons Obamacare Is a Failure,* ThoughtCo. (2017). Article. Web.

[51] Feldpausch, Sarah, *Six Years on Obamacare Has Failed to Deliver,* Americans for Tax Reform, (2016). Article. Web.

[52] Ibid.

President Obama did strongly believe that access to healthcare is a fundamental right. He was convinced that it was the role; and even the duty of the government to subsidize healthcare to the citizen so that those who cannot afford a private insurance could have an alternative one. That is why he enforced his program. According to him [President Obama], the Affordable Care Act would be the steppingstone that would pave the way towards a universal, nationalized, single-payer healthcare system managed and supplied by the federal government. Nonetheless, to say that access to healthcare is a fundamental right, suggests that the government has a central role to play in the attribution of that right.

The problem with that statement though, is that rights are not the government's prerogative to give[53] to the individual. The role of the government is only to protect rights that already exist. Not to create new rights. John Locke wrote about inalienable rights: God-given rights that cannot be taken away[54] by any external entity or exogenic force such as a government. Locke considered the right to life, liberty and property to be among such natural rights.[55] The rights to life, liberty and property are also considered as negative rights because they are natural rights. They are rights that can only be enforced. The individual cannot be deprived of these rights. The reason why access to healthcare is not a fundamental right; is because it is a derivative right that is already part of the right to life. Since health is an

---

[53] Baum, Caroline, *Why Healthcare Is Not A Right.* Economics21. (2015). Article. Web.

[54] Ibid.
[55] Ibid.

inclusive and intrinsic part of life, the two cannot be separated into two distinctive rights. The individual is the master and responsible for his life. Thus, it is the responsibility of the individual to maintain his condition within the scope of his abilities. Of course, there are hereditary diseases that man cannot necessarily control. That is why man has the ability to rely on the market to find new solutions that would ameliorate his living condition. Access to healthcare is not a right because it is not a natural entitlement. Making access to healthcare a full and idiosyncratic entitlement when it is actually not; it is to empower the government to control prices and production of medical supplies; to manage medical resources and to determine the terms and conditions under which an individual is eligible to have access to healthcare. A system like the single-payer system is a system in which the individual who is also the patient and the consumer, is deprived of choosing the medical plan that best fits his medical needs. He is constrained to abide by an incomplete and flawed healthcare plan that would contain several loopholes and inadequate provisions. The Affordable Care Act was exactly this foretaste of what the healthcare system would be like if it were solely run by the federal government.

Like President Obama, Senator Bernie Sanders is deeply convinced of the effectiveness of his want-to-be program "Medicare-For-All," which is properly known as the single-payer system. Senator Sanders has vehemently defended his plan by relying on social democracies such as those of Continental Europe, and more specifically those of the Scandinavian countries; as a model where the universal healthcare system works effectively. He has always taken Sweden as an example to support his theory. However, there are two fundamental flaws in the Senator's argument, which clearly preclude the efficiency of the single-payer system. The first predicament in his argument is grounded in the fact that Sweden and the United States have neither the same density population nor the same socioeconomic realities. Sweden is a country of approximately ten million inhabitants with a homogeneous culture. The cultural factors such as ethnicity, language, tradition and religion; are uniformed and standardized in Sweden. The United States, on the other hand, has a population of over 300 million inhabitants with a culturally diversified national population, which means that the socioeconomic conditions that every community goes through is different from one another. It is subsequently easier for the Swedish government to supply healthcare to its citizens. The swedes have agreed to pay higher taxes in exchange for healthcare security. Conversely, Sweden did not escape the scourge of socialized medicine. Swedish law stipulates that patients should wait no more than 90 days to undergo surgery or see a specialist.[56] Yet every third patient waits longer, according to government figures—patients must also see a general practitioner within seven days, second-longest deadline in Europe after Portugal.[57] Swedes also complain not being able to see their own regular general practitioner—and ensuing lack of continuity—as a growing number of doctors and nurses are temporary hires employed by staffing

---

[56] Editors, *Swedes face problems with healthcare system.* The Business Times. (2018). Article. Web.

[57] Ibid.

companies.[58] Before the utopian project got under way, Sweden had some of the absolute lowest taxes in the civilized world and, not surprisingly, was ranked at the top in terms of standard of living.[59] The socialized medicine project changed Sweden into a country with the second highest tax rate in the world after Denmark, periods of rampant inflation and a steadily deteriorating economy.[60] A huge bureaucracy has been erected to take on all the necessary central planning of public and pseudo-private healthcare.[61] The public healthcare system has expanded while private doctors lose patients because the service is free so everyone wants to benefit from it. Free goods

---

[58] Ibid.

[59] Bernpaintner, Klaus, *The Truth About Sweden Care,* Mises Institute, (2013). Article. Web.

[60] Ibid.
[61] Ibid.

imply higher demand and shortage of supply. Higher demand means increasing the price of goods and services in order to maintain the supply of those goods or services. Swedish doctors are then forced to abandon their profession in the private sector in order to work in the public sector so that they could meet ends need. In 2004, Sweden spent about 9.1. percent of its GDP on healthcare, which is slightly above the average for nations that belong to the Organization of Economic Cooperation and Development (OECD).[62]

If we were to have a single-payer system in the United States, the average American citizen will have a substantial amount of his income automatically deducted from his

---

[62] Hogberg, David, *Sweden's Single-Payer Health System Provides A Warning to Other Nations.* National Center for Public Policy Research. (2007). Article.

paycheck for healthcare expenditures by the federal government. Senator Sanders wants us to spend more than we can afford. The second predicament in Senator Sanders' argument is that if the single-payer system was invigorated as the national healthcare program, the federal government will command state governments to abide by this new law. Since federal law overrides state law, each state will be compelled to impose a mandatory healthcare system upon its citizens whether the state government independently agrees or not. Therefore, the citizen will be paying double taxes on healthcare; state tax and federal tax. The single-payer system will reflect a significant encroachment on state's rights if it were enforced as law of the land. It is important to understand that the government is naturally inclined to mismanage the resources that it is in charge of, for the simple reason that central planners lack crucial information that is needed to incentivize innovation.

The socialized part of our healthcare system has already been proven to be a disaster. Medicare and Medicaid cost more than they worth. The number of participants in Medicare and Medicaid continues to grow as their costs concomitantly augment as well; and the quality of their service remain poor. Obamacare has followed the same principles of socialized medicine. It is more expensive to the taxpayer and delivers a poor quality of medical attention. Funding programs based on emotional decision always lead to detrimental consequences in the long run because these decisions are not processed thoroughly. Having a universal or single-payer healthcare system only subsidized by the federal government where everyone has access to; sounds just, fair, reasonable, and delivers short-termed gains. But in the long run, like any industry that a central authority is in charge of; it will be eventually mismanaged and will deliver adverse effects on the national population overall.

Free healthcare always sounds good at first but always end up becoming deficient then harmful. The American people shall seriously think thorough this temptation. Politicians like Senator Sanders are selling illusions to the American people; making them believe that healthcare is a right although it is not. The American people shall not give government the power to regulate the medical industry. A market-based healthcare system gives more opportunities to the average man to choose the healthcare plan that adequately fits the needs of his medical condition, and to have the ability to purchase the new medical products that the market has to offer. Embracing a socialized healthcare system is taking the path toward serfdom.

4.

The Progressive Income Taxation Must Be Reformed

A progressive income taxation is a form of fiscal policy that the federal government uses to stimulate the economy. It imposes a higher rate on the wealthy than on the poor and it is based on the taxpayer's ability to pay.[63] The progressive income tax system, for example, taxes low-income taxpayers at 10 percent; middle-income taxpayers at 15 percent and

---

[63] Amadeo, Kimberly, *Progressive Taxes With Examples: How a Progressive Tax System Helps the Economy.* The Balance. (2019). Article. Web.

high-income taxpayers at 30 percent.[64] It evidently seems fair because it enables those in the low-income class to spend less in taxation. The system of progressive taxation wants to illuminate itself before the average American citizen; that by taxing more the rich, it is doing justice to everyone while it is surely not the case.

The progressive income tax system derives from the Marxist concept of exploitation of the bourgeoisie class over the proletarian class. It should not be forgotten that during the nineteenth century, the idea that the rich exploited the labor of the poor, had become the dominant political thought in Continental Europe and in the United Kingdom. The socialist movement led by Eugene Debs and Herbert

---

[64] "Theme 3: Fairness in Taxes: Lesson 3: Progressive Taxes", *Understanding Taxes.* Internal Revenue Service. Article.

Croly on the other side of the Atlantic, became also a prominent idea for all those American who resented a complete laissez-faire economy. The progressive income taxation had become the economic doctrine for egalitarian believers. To them, such a system could mitigate the exploitation of the rich upon the poor.

The progressive income tax may sound fair and may promote economic justice in theory, but there is a real problem with its functioning. One of the major downsides of progressive taxation is that it inherently discourages people from working harder and becoming more successful.[65] With a progressive tax bracket, additional monetary benefits are diluted with higher taxes, and at some point people may come to the decision that making more money is

---

[65] McDaniel, Mario, *The Disadvantages of Progressive Taxes.* Pocket Sense. (2017). Article. Web.

not worthwhile because of the high rates.[66] It is said that the main benefit of having a progressive taxation system is that it reduces the income inequality gap. According to economist Roger A. Arnold, excessive inequality can lead to political instability.[67] By shifting the wealth of the society, the progressive tax system helps reduce inequality.[68] According to a study conducted by the Tax Policy Center in 2018, households in the lowest income quintile have a negative federal income tax rates if they receive refundable tax credits.[69] Although the working-class pays less in federal taxes; states taxes, however, have replaced the federal

---

[66] Ibid.

[67] Wolfe, Michelle, *Advantages and Disadvantages of Progressive Tax.* Sapling. (2011). Article. Web.

[68] Ibid.

[69] Staff, "Key Elements of the U.S. Tax System." *Tax Policy Center Briefing Book.* Tax Policy Center. (2018). Article.

burden in taxation. According to a study conducted by the Institute on Taxation and Economic Policy; in 2015 the poorest fifth of Americans will be paying on average 10.9 percent of their income in state and local taxes, the middle fifth will be paying 9.4 percent and the top 1 percent will be paying 5.4 percent under a regressive income tax if the progressive income tax was not enforced.[70] Under the current system of taxation in the United States, about 47 percent of people do not pay any taxes.[71]

The goal of a progressive tax system is to create a system of fairness where everyone pays their "fair share" but the reality of such system is that many households pay more than

---

[70] Cohen, Patricia, *Study Finds Local Taxes Hit Lower Wage Earners Harder,* The New York Times. (2015). Article. Web.

[71] Ayres, Crystal, *11 Biggest Progressive Tax Pros and Cons.* Vittana Personal Finance Blog. . Article. Web.

they should because many pay nothing.[72] The progressive tax system does not promote any economic justice for the simple reason that it penalizes the wealthy, which means those who have the ability to create employment and wealth are precluded to do so. Making the rich paying more than they should; is making a disservice to them. The "rich," as most people want to pejoratively categorize the ones who belong to a high-income threshold; are the people who truly stimulate the market and the economy as a whole. For an economy to thoroughly advance, it is imperative that those who have the means to advance and to create wealth, have to the freedom to do so. The creation of wealth is primarily based on human capital. Without human capital, there is no productivity and without productivity there is no

---

[72] Ibid.

creation of wealth. A progressive income tax makes it harder for those who have the means to create wealth to actually do so because the federal government arbitrarily deprives them to use their wealth into productive ventures that would uplift more people from poverty.

A flat income tax system shall be reinstated as the main tax system of the United States. The flat tax system is the fairest and most equitable system in which individuals are truly equal in the payment of their fair share. Not equal in the amount of taxes that each of them must pay, but equal in the percentage that everyone shall have to pay. The flat income tax gives a fix rate that everyone shall be paying.

For everyone to truly benefit from a flat income tax system, the budget of the federal government must be fully reduced. It suggests that the federal government must abolish many federal agencies such as the Department of Education, privatizing the Social Security Administration, abolishing the Environmental and Protection Agency, the Department of Housing and many other unnecessary departments that are only embellishing and amplifying the power of the federal government as well as the rate of taxes that the taxpayer is compelled to pay. A flat tax would get rid of the whole enormously complicated tax code administered by the Internal Revenue Service.[73] This would not only save the government the cost of running an unnecessarily huge bureaucracy, it would save the country as a whole the enormous costs of supporting a whole industry of tax accountants.[74] Moreover, the

---

[73] Sowell, Thomas, *The Many Benefits of a Flat Tax.* St. Louis Post-Dispatch. (1996).

[74] Ibid.

economy would also benefit because everyone would have more incentive to work and produce.[75] The progressive tax system does not benefit anyone, especially not the working-class. It only benefits the federal government itself because this system allows it to create more federal agencies. We shall not forget that any federal agency is always created by the taxpayer's money. On the other hand, the flat tax system forces the federal government to shrink its size as well as its power to the benefit of the taxpayer.

---

[75] Ibid.

5.

Political Correctness:
A Serious Impediment To Free
Speech

In the elaboration of the civil liberties that encapsulate the ten first amendments to the United States Constitution, also known as the Bill of Rights, the right to free speech is, indeed, a component of the First Amendment to the Constitution. What does free speech mean and why is it so important for the sustentation of our republic? The free speech clause stipulates that:

"Congress shall make no law respecting an establishment of religion or prohibiting the free exercise thereof; or abridging the freedom of

speech, or of the press; or the right of the people peaceably to assemble, and to petition the Government for a redress of grievances."[76]

The primary objective of a liberal democracy is to ensconce the rights of the individual, which means to protect the rights of the individual by the application of the law. The first prerequisite for a liberal democracy to function is to enable the individual to assert his opinion over the management of public affairs. The freedoms of speech, press, assembly and the right to petition the government and seek redress of grievances proclaim that citizens have the right to call the government to account.[77] Freedoms of speech and press allow citizens to communicate their ideas verbally and in writing, while freedom of

---

[76] "The Constitution of the United States," Amendment 1.

[77] "U.S. Institutions–Why is the First Amendment Important?" *Ideals and Institutions.* Editorials. (2017). Article. Web.

assembly lets them publicly express a common interest.[78] The right to petition allows citizens to point out to the government where it did not follow the law, to seek changes, as well as damages for such missteps.[79] For the Founding Fathers, freedom of expression whether it is free speech, the right to assemble or the right to petition; is indeed the social tool that would constrain the power of the federal government. The whole freedom of expression contrivance was intended to thwart the federal government from arbitrarily expanding its power without providing any form of legitimate justification.

In authoritarian and totalitarian states such as the People's Republic of China, the Federative Republic of Russia, Eastern European countries, Cuba, Northern African

---

[78] Ibid.
[79] Ibid.

countries, Middle Eastern countries, and most African countries; freedom of expression is merely a rhetorical right rather than an actual concrete constitutional right. But the peoples in these countries have never seen this right being enforced to their benefits. Instead, the peoples in these countries have been deprived of this right. In China for instance, free speech is not a right but a privilege. Chinese authorities, recognizing in recent years that limited freedom of expression enables the government to better monitor potentially problematic social issues; have begun to tolerate criticism; but only from certain categories of people, a kind of "free-speech elite," and only then in government-controlled forums.[80] The only people in China

---

[80] Representative James P. McGovern and Senator Marco Rubio, "Freedom of Expression in China: A Privilege, Not a Right." *Congressional-Executive Commission on China.* Article.

who can publish criticism of, or opinions contrary to those of the Communist Party, are senior members of the Communist Party, intellectuals and professional elite, linguistic elite, and financial elite. Academics and editors are allowed to publicly question government policies, and even to criticize them in private.[81] The operative principle with respect to this group could express as follows: the degree to which the Chinese government is willing to tolerate criticism of its leaders and policies is contingent upon the size and nature of the audience and the ideological credentials of the speaker.[82] This operative principle acutely demonstrates that freedom of expression in the People's Republic of China is an extrinsically conditioned freedom that only members of a

---

[81] Ibid.
[82] Ibid.

certain social class have the right to enjoy. Free speech, as we understand it in liberal democracies, is clearly not applicable in totalitarian states like China. The ordinary citizen's opinion weights no value. He is not allowed to express his opinion or to hold the Chinese government accountable for its action. If he dared to speak or to express his opinion, he will be subsequently punished by the government. It is preponderant to note that liberal democracies such as the United States, France, Canada, or the United Kingdom; have begun to adopt a censorship policy like in China, where freedom of expression is becoming more and more restricted to ordinary citizens or individuals who do not embrace a particular ideology. And this restriction of freedom of expression that emerged in our democracies is called political correctness.

Political correctness is the avoidance, often considered as taken to extremes, of forms of expression or action that are perceived to exclude, marginalize, or insult groups of people who are socially disadvantaged or discriminated against. According to the *Merriam-Webster Dictionary,* political correctness is the act of conforming to a belief that language and practices which could offend political sensibilities should be eliminated.[83] At first glance, political correctness seems to be a means of ensconcing more equality between individuals, especially by helping those who are marginalized. But in reality, political correctness is indeed a detrimental element for American society because it forces those who do not agree with the mainstream discourse, to accept it without concessions. Political correctness has

---

[83] "Politically Correct" *Merriam-Webster.*

become the tool whereby the federal government controls the narrative of the mainstream culture. It is the new form of totalitarianism that has transpired in America because the government uses language as an instrument to control what is "politically correct" from what it is not. It dictates what is appropriate from what it is not. Thus, political correctness subverts the First Amendment, and particularly the right to free speech. In October 2017, the Cato Institute released a national poll that found an astounding 71 percent of Americans who believe that political correctness is silencing discussions society needs to have, while 58 percent said they have political views they are afraid to share.[84] The majority of Democrats (53 percent) said that they did not

---

[84] Wagoner, Josh, *How Political Correctness and Identity Politics Are Destroying America.* The Daily Caller. (2018). Article. Web.

feel the need to self-censor, while a super majority of Republicans (73 percent) and Independents (58 percent) felt the need to keep some political beliefs to themselves.[85] What has truly generated political correctness in America is identity politics.

Identity politics claims oppressive forces such as racism and sexism virtually dominate our political and social institutions.[86] While no society can live on bigotry outright, identity politics ignores the reality that America has advanced individual rights as equalities farther than any nation.[87] It is imperative to say that political correctness serves the cause of a political ideology at the expense of the collective consciousness. Political correctness serves the cause of left-wing movements such

---

[85] Ibid.
[86] Ibid.
[87] Ibid.

as progressivism, and social democracies that rely on cultural Marxism to not only dismantle culture, but to also impose their regressive and resentful views of the world on American society. Progressive parties everywhere have sought to monopolize educational and cultural institutions in order to force those under their thumbs to sing their tunes or to shut up.[88] Political correctness is mostly used at universities by left-wing professors and Marxist intellectuals who are imposing their way of thinking upon students. And students are compelled to abide by it, or they would face severe consequences. Conservative students are shut off from the public discourse for their political views and their First Amendment right is daily violated. The federal government does

---

[88] Codevilla, Angelo, *The Rise of Political Correctness,* Independent Institute. (2016). Article. Web.

nothing to protect those whose First Amendment rights are constantly violated whether it is at universities or even in the workplace. The way in which the government uses political correctness to control the public discourse is that it switches from what is considered to be incorrect as hateful. When a speech is considered or declared as hate speech because it discomforts the general discourse; the government subsequently intervenes to regulate the narrative. This, therefore, empowers the government to determine words that enter into the lexicon of political correctness. It has been the case in countries like Australia or Canada. Nonetheless, hate speech is not yet regulated in America but it is regulated in most liberal democracies. It is a matter of time before the federal government expands its power over the

First Amendment and begins to regulate free speech.

The problem of political correctness is not solely scoped in America. It has become an epidemy that has spread throughout the West. In Canada, for example, it has become a serious issue. When the state gains the power to outlaw certain forms of expression such as "hate speech"; the result is rarely a decrease in hate but always expanded power of grotesque new forms of bureaucratic busybodying.[89] Canadians do not enjoy a universal right to speech; expressing and consuming certain ideas and opinions is regulated by law.[90] This is rationalized by the Canadian constitution's declaration that government has a right to

---

[89] McCullough, J.J. *How Canada Bans Books.* National Review. (2018). Article. Web.

[90] Ibid.

restrain freedoms with "reasonable limits prescribed by law as can be demonstrated and justified in a free and democratic society."[91] The right to restrain free speech means the right to ban book that could convey hateful thoughts. Section 319 of the Criminal Code of Canada says:

"Everyone who, by communicating statements, other than in private conversation, willfully promotes hatred against identifiable group is guilty of

(a) An indictable offence and is liable to imprisonment for a term not exceeding two years; or

(b) An offence punishable on summary conviction."[92]

The Canadian government retains more power to regulate the national language, which is a dangerous boon for any kind of government to

---

[91] Ibid.
[92] Ibid.

become more centralized, powerful and totalitarian. The United States government is surely an already powerful government that controls most aspects of the American way of life, but it has not dared yet to officially implement hate speech laws because it would be a direct violation of the First Amendment to the Constitution of the United States of America. Left-wing politicians want to use the federal government to make laws that will aim to fully control by decree if necessary, the mainstream narrative. Interestingly, it is important to know that the federal government had already started the project of changing the language by implementing new words in the lexicon. For example, President Obama passed Rosa's Law, which empowered the federal government to switch the words "mental retardation" to "intellectually challenged" or "intellectually disabled"; although "mental retardation" is not in itself a pejorative word. From now on, it has become imperative that everyone use these words imposed by the federal government. This is one crucial example that exhibits how the government progressively takes control over the use of language and becomes totalitarian in the end. It is tacit totalitarianism in the making.

6.

Fiscal Policy To Control the Economy

Fiscal policy refers to the use of government spending and tax policies to influence economic conditions, including demand for goods and services, employment, inflation and economic growth.[93] Fiscal policy originated from the ideas of one of the most prominent economists of the twentieth century; John Maynard Keynes. In other words, fiscal policy is informally called Keynesian economics to an extent.

---

[93] Kenton, Will, *Fiscal Policy,* Investopedia, Updated in May 2019.

John Maynard Keynes argued that the government is a necessary and unavoidable agent to restore full employment in a country following an economic recession. His theory principally stipulates that aggregate demand is influenced by a host of economic decisions that produce output and inflation.[94] Fiscal policy gives more flexibility to the federal government over the control of price of goods and services. The primary economic impact of any change in the government budget is felt by particular groups—a tax cut for families with children, for example, raises their disposable income.[95] In an open economy, fiscal policy also affects the exchange rate and the trade balance.[96] During

---

[94] Blinder, Alan S. *Keynesian Economics*. The Library of Economics and Liberty. Article. Web.

[95] Weil, David, N. *Fiscal Policy*. The Library of Economics and Liberty. Article.

[96] Ibid.

times of economic recession, the federal government uses fiscal expansionary policy, which means that the federal government raises the interest rates due to government borrowing to attract foreign capital.[97] The goal behind the fiscal expansionary policy is to expand the money supply in the economy so that people will have more money to spend. During times of economic expansion, the government uses a fiscal contractionary policy. The purpose of contractionary fiscal policy is to slow growth to a healthy economic level, which is generally between 2 and 3 percent a year.[98] Regardless of the policy used, the federal government retains much power over the economic activities being produced and that is a problem.

---

[97] Ibid.

[98] Amadeo, Kimberly, *Contractionary Fiscal Policy and Its Purpose With Examples.* The Balance. (2019). Article. Web.

I do personally believe that the use of fiscal policy is generally a problem rather than a remedy because it allows the government to, not only control economic resources, but to also control the quantity of money supply although the Federal Reserve is the institution in charge of supplying money to the economy. The federal government can control money supply through fiscal means rather than monetary means because the government has the ability to infinitely borrow. This infinite access to the borrowing of money, empowers the federal government to determine how much money is needed from the Federal Reserve. This is a method in which the federal government ensures to ascertain its control over economic policy and to further its totalitarian rule upon the people.

The central problem of fiscal policy is that it accelerates inflation rate. Indeed, the rate of inflation increases because the federal government has the ability to print more money than it is necessary. Inflation surges with the quantity of money that the government has printed and has put into circulation. The increase in inflation rate means that taxes have to also increase in order to maintain a certain equilibrium. Since the government can generate income only through the collection of taxes to subsidize its programs; it, therefore, increases the rate of inflation in order to deduce more taxes from the taxpayer's income. Furthermore, bureaucrats in Washington argue that a fiscal policy is necessary to redistribute the wealth, and to alleviate poverty. But the redistribution of wealth through government means has only provided short-term benefits. In the first chapter of this book, I have demonstrated how government social welfare programs adversely affect low-income families who are dependent upon these programs. The government also uses the progressive income tax system to subsidize its social welfare programs, which I also explained in the fourth chapter. Using the progressive income tax system to subsidize means-tested programs inevitably result in an escalation of inflation.

In today's America, albeit the federal government does not control the economy through a command-style; it still controls all of the economic activities through arbitrary rules and regulations on businesses. It gives an edge to bureaucrats in Washington to control the economy without necessarily understanding all the factors involved which determine the motion of the economy as a whole. Fiscal policy is the economic tool that legitimizes the legal totalitarianism of the federal government over the national population. The technocrats settled in Washington; those who are utterly disconnected from the real world and from the daily struggles of the ordinary citizens; are the ones who determine the poverty threshold in America. According to the U.S. Bureau Census in 2018, the poverty line in the United States is $13, 064.00 for an individual under the age of 65, and $12, 043 for any individual who is 65 years of age and beyond.[99] For two people living together in the same household and filing taxes jointly and who are under 65, the poverty line is set at $16,815. For two individuals over 65, the poverty line is determined at $15,178.[100] This is in the case for no children living with them. If we compare the living standard of the United States and that of Mexico, we can all agree that

---

[99] Poverty Thresholds for 2018. Data.

[100] Ibid.

they can never be the same simply because the United States has a better GDP than that of Mexico. Moreover, both currencies do not have the same value. Consequently, a middle-class man from Mexico who moves to the United States; will be relegated to the working-class in America because the living standard is higher in the United Sates since it is based on the rate of inflation. It means that the inflation rate elevates the living standard and the poverty threshold increases as the living standard increases. Conversely, those living in the poverty threshold in America would surely be in the upper-class if they were living in Mexico. The point behind this argument is to authenticate that; by using fiscal policy, the United States government is the one responsible for the incrementation of the inflation rate as well as the enlargement of poverty.

The best way to constrain the power of the federal government over the economy is by the use of monetary policy over fiscal policy. Since inflation is the central element that determines certain economic factors such as supply and demand, prices and interest rates; monetary policy aims to keep inflation relatively low as the gold standard did it during the first quarter of the twentieth century. Milton Friedman, who was one of the foremost economists in American history, has vividly advocated for the use of monetary policy to contain inflation. Monetary policy involves influencing the demand and supply of money, primarily through the use of interest rates.[101] Raising interest rates is usually quite effective

---

[101] Pettinger, Tejvan, *Monetary Policy vs Fiscal Policy.* Economics Help. (2018).. Article. Web.

in reducing inflationary pressures.[102] Real interest rates affect the cost of capital; the cost of capital affects capital accumulation; the capital stock affects the demand for labor; the demand for labor affects unemployment.[103]

The use of contractionary monetary policy also reduces the quantity of money supply at a reasonable rate, which subsequently reduces inflation from increasing. Less money in circulation will surely reduce the purchasing power of the consumer but prices will also fall. It is, nonetheless, preponderant to fathom that this decrease is to alleviate short-term interest rates. An economy is healthy when its inflation rate gradually increases by a two percent margin. Inflation must increase so that it keeps

---

[102] Ibid.

[103] Blanchard, Olivier, "2. Monetary policy affects both the actual and the natural rate of unemployment." *Monetary Policy and Unemployment*. (2003). Article.

the economy moving, but it should increase reasonably so that unemployment does not skyrocket. If inflation grows faster than its long-trend, which means between 3 and 10 percent a year, it becomes alarming because prices of goods and services and wages substantially increase above the nominal rate. Inflation in that percentage bracket (3-10 percent) concurrently incentivizes unemployment rate to go higher. The use of monetary policy allows businesses to exert more leverage in the economy because there is less pressure from the government to adjust prices as well as supply and demand, and therefore to maintain unemployment rate low. When prices are determined by businesses rather than by the government through the policy of aggregate supply; it substantiates that these businesses know better than anyone the needs of the consumer and can adequately adjust their price to rationally stimulate demand. The supply and demand ration established by a business thus promulgates price stability. Price stability helps businesses, households, and financial institutions to make better decision, thereby fostering the stability of the financial system.[104]

Monetary policy and fiscal policy do have the same goals which are; the sustentation of positive economic growth (long-run trend rate of 2.5 percent), full employment, the maintenance of inflation at a low level.[105] The principal aim of fiscal and monetary policy is to reduce cyclical fluctuations in the economic

[104] Mester, Loretta J., *Five Points About Monetary Policy and Financial Stability*. The Federal Reserve Bank of Cleveland. (2016). Article.

[105] Pettinger, Tejvan, *Monetary policy vs. Fiscal Policy*. Economic Help. (2018). Article. Web.

cycle.[106] Between the two, monetary policy is the most effective policy to attenuate inflation because it does not require government intervention. Today, a central bank is deemed necessary to fulfill that task; not the government. A central bank, in this case which is the Federal Reserve; has to raise interest rates in order to bring inflation down. Increasing interest rates also increases the cost of borrowing and increasing the cost of borrowing discourages spending. The problem with central banks such as the Federal Reserve, is that it monopolizes the supply of money and implements policies though that benefits the government rather than the people. These policies do considerably augment the influence of the government over our lives. The wars in which the United States have been involved,

---

[106] Ibid.

were primarily supplied by the central bank. The central bank, although it is the institution that is in charge of the maintaining inflation low, works hand in hand with the government to amplify the power of the state over the people. The central bank of the United States, which is the Federal Reserve for that matter, shall be abolished. It should be abolished because centralizing monetary policy is one of the factors that creates economic crises and it is a form of totalitarianism over the supply of money. It is important and even judicious that monetary policy is conducted by state and local banks rather than a central bank that would monopolize the supply of money and implement the wrong policies. Localism is the political foundation of the United States. By keeping civil policy local, including monetary policy, the people would subsequently exert more control over their lives and over the government than the government would over them. So long as the United States government will keep using fiscal policy to control the economy, its power will continue to self-aggrandize while the freedom of the people will continue to shrink to the point of no return. Then, the totalitarianism of the federal government will be absolute over us.

7.

Social Justice
Does No Justice

Social justice has been a recurring subject, or should I say, a repetitive issue brought up in the political discourse; especially after the Second World War; when most Westerners began to embrace social liberalism, social democracy, socialism, and central planning.

The concept of social justice took officially shape in America when the welfare state was introduced and implemented in the 1930s. It is preponderant to comprehend that social justice is nothing else than a mere economic justice, or the quest for a fair redistribution of resources. The word "social" is used to give more magnitude, and especially to accentuate on the moral aspect of the redistribution of wealth. The concept of social justice is based on morality to justify the redistribution of wealth. Albeit, the problem with social justice is that the government is used as the great equalizer to spread the wealth. Using the government as the great equalizer hints that coercion would be legitimized to enforce equality, and such method only benefits the government to become more and more powerful while the rights of the citizen are considerably and progressively shrinking.

The use of morality in order to justify the enforcement of equality by government means; signifies that the government has the legitimacy to deprive an individual of his rights and property, arbitrarily, for the sake of enabling the disenfranchised to have access to those resources. If the state can only give to Peter what it takes away from Paul, it is afterward immoral to confiscate the property of Paul and supply it to Peter on the mere basis that it will be fairer and just for Peter because Peter does not have access to it. Using morality to enforce equality does not right the wrong. In fact, it enlarges the inequality gap. Egalitarians have always refused to perceive inequality as a natural phenomenon of the human condition. Yet it is. The human race was conceived in poverty. Even the Bible has made it clear. Adam had to work tremendously hard to provide for his family. Wealth has simply been created between humans by voluntary exchanges of goods and services that mutually benefit the two parties partaking into that transaction. Each party then made profit by producing a greater output from the transaction they have benefited from. This output produced is what we know in economic term as capital. This is how capital was created and so the first men generated material wealth.

Intellectuals who advocate for egalitarianism have never sought to know what creates wealth. They are just interested in how to redistribute it. They use factors such as genetics and the environment to justify economic disparities between the haves and the have-nots. According to them, the poor are poor because they either come from lagging social and ethnic groups whose IQ is genetically claimed to be lower than the nominal standard, which means that they are not and will never be good in school; or they live in hostile environment where economic opportunities are significantly scarce. Egalitarian intellectuals, therefore, argue that the poor can never become rich on their own because they lack the means to do so. They consequently maintain that it is the moral duty of the federal government to intervene and to provide for them. For example, egalitarian intellectuals contend that Affirmative Action is a necessary policy that should be upheld on the premise that it gives a chance to African American students, who mostly come from lagging social groups, to attend a good academic institution and to receive a good education. They justify their stance on the ground that the legacy of slavery has prevented most African Americans to have access to opportunities that their white counterparts have. However, egalitarian intellectuals vehemently refuse to acknowledge that economic disparities are not due to genetic or environmental factors, nor to discrimination but it is due to cultural factors. As a matter of fact, the cultural factor plays a substantive role in the economic achievement of social groups. There is a myth that says that the Jewish community is the most economically successful community because their people are the smartest. Notwithstanding the fact that economic success requires some degree of intelligence, the Jewish community is not the most economically successful community because of their intelligence. Jewish people are successful in America simply because of the cultural value that they have attached to education, family, and hard work when they settled in the United States. For example, when the U.S. Army gave mental test to its soldiers during the First World War, soldiers of Scottish ancestry scored above the average of white draftees, while soldiers from groups that had emigrated from Poland and Russia—mostly Jews—scored below that average.[107] Did that mean that the Scots were more intelligent than the Jews? Or did it mean that a group whose peak immigration years were generations earlier than the Jews' peak immigration years, and who spoke English even before arriving in the United States from Scotland, could understand mental test questions and test instructions written in English better than people who grew up in homes where English was not usually the language spoken?[108] With the passing years as more American Jews grew up speaking English, their IQ test scores rose above the national average.[109] As their English became significantly better over time, American Jews began to have more economic opportunities available to them. They were

---

[107] Sowell, Thomas, "Social Factors," *Wealth, Poverty and Politics*. Basic Books. (2016). ISBN: 978-0-465-09676-3. P. 164. Print.
[108] Ibid. p. 164.
[109] Ibid. p. 164.

performing all kinds of job from menial works to highly intellectual endeavors. They created new venues in certain industries that did previously not exist. How were the Jews able to do that? Simply by being culturally receptive to the customs of the country in which they were living in. Another example can be introduced to solidify the case on cultural values as a decisive factor in economic achievement. If native-born Americans who are in lower income brackets do not move up nearly as often as immigrants who arrived in those same lower income brackets— the Chinese and the Cubans for example—then the question must be raised whether there external barriers to mobility blocking the rise of native-born Americans—barriers which somehow exempt immigrants.[110] A more realistic explanation might be that low-income

---

[110] "Population" Ibid. p. 181.

immigrants bring a different set of attitudes and values than the attitudes and values of native-born low-income Americans.[111] And this fundamental difference is based on the sentiment of entitlement. Low-income immigrants do not feel entitled because they are very well aware that there is no one to give them what they need except putting their skills to work in order to obtain economic progress while low-income native-born Americans do feel entitled because they have social welfare programs at their disposal and from which they benefit anytime they want.

Social justice is an actual impediment to acquiring human capital because it prevents those at the ladder to be economically emancipated. The concept psychologically misguides them by making the have-nots

---

[111] "Population" Ibid. p. 181.

believing that the reason why they do not have access to the tools necessary to have a better life condition is because someone else took those tools away from them. Although it is clearly not the case. This attitude makes those in lagging groups more resentful and culturally unreceptive towards the groups that are economically more successful than them. Since these lagging groups feel materially dispossessed, they do not see why they should be making so much effort to be at the same level as those who are economically advanced. They believe that it is the role of the government to provide for them. The concept of social justice merely empowers the federal government to retain full control over human capital in lagging groups. What people in lagging groups do not grasp is that the essence of wealth does come from nowhere else but human capital. Human capital is simply the set of human knowledge, skills, abilities and talents that individuals put to use to create output. Anyone can do so because any individual has a set of skills that he or she can be put to use and subsequently increase his or her output.

Social justice keeps widening the inequality gap because the government intervenes in the redistribution of the allocation of resources. Those who receive government handouts based on the premise that these handouts "help them to achieve self-sufficiency" is undeniably erred. It keeps them in a state of poverty and does no justice to them. Indeed, social justice does no justice to those it intends to help but instead, keeps them at the bottom of the social ladder. If we take a close look at our educational system, we can clearly see that the federal government being in charge of our educational system; has created more socioeconomic disparities. The Department of Education was created in the late 1970s with, of course, the best of intentions. These intentions were to ensure that individuals from lagging groups would have access to an education regardless of their socioeconomic status. In order to uphold that principle, the federal government has imposed the Common Core system. The Common Core system is a system designed to impose a uniform; standardized curriculum that every state-owned school is required to administer to its students. The ideology behind the effectuation of the Common Core system is the enforcement of egalitarianism; which means that all students; regardless of their race, religion, ethnic background, and economic status; are all equal in learning the same subjects incorporated in a national curriculum. Nonetheless, the Common Core system does not enhance the readiness of the students and does not equate students of different social backgrounds to the same level. It is merely a tool for the state to enlarge the power of the government over the school system. The heart of Common Core is the centralization of decision-making in education. One problem with centralization is that it removes parents from the decision-making process[112] regarding the welfare of their own children. In the early days of public education, parents were involved in decision about hiring and firing teachers, retaining local control over their local schools.[113] As public schools grew

---

[112] Courtney, Jennifer, *Problems with Common Core that Need Attention,* Classical Conversations. Classical Christian Community. (2019). Article. Web.

[113] Ibid.

larger, the levels of bureaucracy also aggrandized.[114]

Common Core regulates what needs to be taught and it dictates that students be tested and tracked by the federal government.[115] Common Core is indisputably a form of totalitarianism that the federal government exerts on our educational system to retain full control over the means of production. It does not make students with lower IQs any smarter or more academically proficient. Between 2013 and 2015, the latest data available on Common Core outcomes by the U.S. Department of Education, shows that nationally, teaching Algebra in grade 8 dropped from 33 percent to 29 percent.[116]

---

[114] Ibid.

[115] Ibid.

[116] Pullman, Joy, *How Common Core Damages Student's College Readiness.* The James G. Martin Center For Academic Renewal. (2017). Article. Web.

These results are largely due to the fact that Common Core degrades the level of expected math completion for high school to a partially completed Algebra II course.[117] According to the Every Student Succeeds Act, even the highest-quality public universities must admit students at this low level of preparation, and place them into "credit-bearing," not remedial coursework.[118] Bureaucrats retain the power to make decisions over the kind of subjects that should be taught to students without even considering the mental capabilities of each of these students. Data from the National Center for Education Statistics shows that in 2017, members from low-income communities such as the African American community or the Hispanic community, have SAT scores lower than their

[117] Ibid.
[118] Ibid.

white and Asian counterparts. The aggregated SAT score for African Americans was 941 and 990 for Hispanics, compare to 1118 for whites and 1181 for Asians.[119] Students from low-income brackets and from minority groups with problematic learning abilities; have trouble performing well at the university level because they are admitted under lower standards and exogenous factors such as race or gender; that have nothing to do with their academic credentials. Their predicament to do well at the university level is not based upon their level of intelligence, but it is based on racial-preferential policies that misplace them in the wrong academic institutions. High-quality universities use affirmative action policies to determine the admission basis of each entering

---

[119] SAT Score Data. (2017).

class. These racial-preferential policies are administered in the admission process in order to enforce "equality of opportunity." These racial-preferential policies focus on admitting non-white students from low-income neighborhoods with low academic credentials. For the social justice advocates, racial-preferential policies are the way to give to the disenfranchised an opportunity to obtain an education. The problem with racial-preferential policies is that it lowers the academic standards of high-quality universities, and the students admitted on those policies, are generally at the bottom of their class because their academic credentials are lower than the general standard of the class. So, the question is, what justice does it do those who gain admission on affirmative action if they are still lagging at the bottom of their class?

The best way to enforce fairness is by letting the market reallocating resources rather than letting the government being in charge of it. Social justice is a mere boon for the consolidation of state authority. Most totalitarian states have an expanded system of social justice. Social justice simply enables government to be in charge of resources that it will eventually mismanage. Social justice does no justice to nobody. The disenfranchised do not suddenly become better-off under social justice policies. Instead, they are still lagging at the bottom because the government makes them feel entitled to receive handouts without having to work for it.

8.

The Militarization of the Police

The police are an entity deeply ingrained in American culture. We mostly cherish it because we have always believed that those who wear the blue uniform, do so voluntarily. They do so because they want to preserve the safety of the community and protect innocent lives. When John Locke articulated in his magnum opus *Second Treatise of Government,* that man is entitled to the right to life, liberty and property, he meant that it was the role of the state to protect that entitlement. One of the ways for the state to protect that entitlement is through the establishment of the police. The right to life entails the enforcement of the protection of that right. Same for the other subsequent ones (liberty and property). That is why, the principle of law and order is an intrinsic part of a free society. We want to be free, but to acquire that freedom, we need law and order in order for each of us to pursue our self-interest. At least, this is the philosophical approach for the necessity of having law enforcement.

Law enforcement has not always been a formal government-run entity in the United States.[120] The early American form of policing was akin to that seen in New England during colonial times, consisting of volunteer groups and privately funded part-time officers.[121]

---

[120] Mosteller, Jeremiah, *The Militarization of Police.* Charles Koch Institute. Article. Web.

[121] Ibid.

Urbanization and the growth of cities resulted in the development of centralized municipal police departments; the first being created by the city of Boston in 1838.[122] Today, there are currently more than 18,000 local, state and federal law enforcement agencies in the United States.[123] These agencies employ over 420,000 law enforcement officers tasked with protecting public safety in our communities.[124] Each year, law enforcement conducts over 10 million arrests, resulting in more than 600,000 admission to state or federal prisons.[125] These activities cost taxpayers over $126 billion each year for federal, state, and local police protection.[126] The police has, indeed, substantially changed from being a mere local

---

[122] Ibid.
[123] Ibid.
[124] Ibid.
[125] Ibid.
[126] Ibid.

entity designed to protect the community into a full military force that appears ready to invade a new territory.

The Police now uses military tactics to apprehend imminent threats. The problem with the militarization of the police is that the government, regardless of the level, authorizes the police to use dangerously unconventional tactics that usually result in a large number of casualties. The increased militarization of the police has occurred alongside a significant decline in public trust for law enforcement agencies.[127] While the public continues to respect their own community's law enforcement agencies, public confidence and trust in law enforcement as an institution has decreased since the early 2000s.[128] The militarization of

---

[127] Ibid.
[128] Ibid.

168

the police neither reduces rates of violent crime nor changes the number of officers assaulted or killed.[129] In fact, the militarization of the police is used, principally but not only, on minority groups such as the Black community or the Hispanic community. In a study conducted by Assistant Professor of Political Science and Public Affairs at Princeton University, Jonathan Mummolo; the report shows that the only concrete result from the militarization of the police is the distrust that the public opinion exerts towards the police as an institution. The study of Dr. Mummolo epitomizes that the militarization of the police principally hurts the Black community the most. As a practical matter, the study substantiates that in the state

---

[129] Akpan, Nsikan, *Police Militarization Fails to Protect Officers and Targets Black Communities, Study Finds.* (2018). Article. Web.

of Maryland for example, a SWAT team was deployed in heavily black-populated areas. Between 2010 and 2014; the SWAT team has been deployed nearly 8200 times to be accurate.[130] The use of SWAT teams to serve warrants, which escalated as a result of the war on drugs, is an extremely disruptive event in the lives of citizens and often involves percussive grenades, battering rams, substantial property damage, and in rare case deadly altercations stemming from citizens' mistaken belief that they are experiencing a home invasion.[131] The routine use of militarized police tactics by local agencies threatens to increase the historic

---

[130] Mummolo, Jonathan, *Militarization Fails to Enhance Police Safety or Reduce Crime but may Harm Police Reputation.* Proceedings of the National Academy of Sciences of the United States of America. (2018). Article.

[131] Ibid.

tensions between marginalized groups and the state, with no detectable public safety benefit.[132]

The militarization of the police is, of course, a bureaucratic policy that only the federal government has the power to either enforce it or to restrain its utilization. Militarizing the police is also ascertaining the totalitarian power of the state. The great interrogation is to know whether our communities really need law enforcement to be necessarily militarized. There is a significant difference between the military and the police. The primary mission of the U.S. military is to destroy the enemies of the nation in battle.[133] The primary mission of American police departments is to protect and serve the

---

[132] Ibid.

[133] Jefferey T. Fowler, Ph.D., *Police Militarization in America— A Negative or Positive Trend?* In Homeland Security. (2017). Article. Web.

communities in which they live.[134] It is very much evident that the military and the police do not serve the same purpose. Having police in military camouflage, carrying military weapons and patrolling in armored or vehicles gives communities the appearance of an armed police confrontation.[135] A research conducted by Edward Lawson Jr. concludes that the militarization of the police is a psychological process that affects individual officers as well as departments.[136] This process involves the adoption of a more militaristic world view, where militarism is the emphasis on the use of force as an acceptable—or even desirable—option to address problems.[137] Militarized police

---

[134] Ibid.

[135] Ibid.

[136] Lawson Jr., Edward. *Evidence Suggests The Militarization of Police Forces Leads To More Civilian Deaths.* LSE US Centre. (2018). Article. Web.

[137] Ibid.

departments see themselves not as public servants upholding the law, but as an army fighting a war against a dangerous and invisible enemy and occupying territory that is hostile to them.[138]

The police are simply militarized because it is in the hand of a central authority. At the outset of this essay, I indicated that the police as an institution, was made up of volunteer groups that were privately funded by the community. That was once upon a time when the people did own the police. Now it has become the opposite. The police own the people. The police do no longer act primarily on behalf of the people but on behalf of the state. The irony is that the goal of the police is to protect the right of the citizens, while in reality, the police has

---

[138] Ibid.

come to violate those same rights.[139] As I have reiterated throughout this book, the government is doomed to mismanage resources, and to always taking it too far. Of course, the government has more means to supply the equipment needed for the police in order to ensure the protection of civilians, compare to if it was privately funded. I have always believed that the police and the military are entities that should be funded by the state because it is the role of the state to secure the rights of its citizens. Yet government is untrustworthy because it always ends up implementing laws which reduce the ability of citizens to retain their own control. The federal government must extensively demilitarize the police in order to

---

[139] Ferrera, Victoria, *Police Militarization in America: The Land of the Free and the Home of Contradictions.* Ramapo College of New Jersey. (2017). Article.

thoroughly preserve the safety and the rights of the citizens. The people must feel empowered and protected by their local police and not the other way around. The discrepancy now established between increasingly militarized police and a disdained community, has widened the mistrust gap between the two. The police as an institution is losing ground in the eyes of the public opinion. The police must be revamped, but it shall be revamped comprehensively with a primacy to emphasize on demilitarizing the police and to give the power back to the community. The continued militarization of the police clearly and limpidly substantiates that we, undeniably, live in a totalitarian state.

9.

The Judicial Activism of the Court

Between the three branches of government, the judicial branch is the most ignored and the most subverted, yet it is the most influential. The American people sometimes do not realize to what extent the Supreme Court, which is the highest court in the land; influences and affects the life of each of us when it renders a legal decision. The Supreme Court of the United States became an equal branch of government following *Marbury v. Madison* in 1803, when the Court has ensconced for the first time the power of judicial review; which is the power of the courts to examine the actions of the other two branches of government and to determine whether such actions are consistent with the Constitution.[140] The power of judicial review has, unequivocally, ascertained the legitimacy of the Supreme Court as well as it has empowered the Court to keep the other two branches in check. The power of the judicial review has, however, generated the concept of judicial activism.

The term *activism* is used in both political rhetoric and academic research.[141] In academic usage, the word "activism" usually means only the willingness of a judge to strike down the action of another branch of government or to

---

[140] Tate, Neal, "Judicial Review," *Law,* Encyclopedia Britannica.

[141] Roosevelt, Kermit, "Judicial Activism," *Law,* Encyclopedia Britannica.

overturn a judicial precedent, with no implied judgment as to whether the activist decision is correct or not.[142] In political rhetoric usage, the word "activism" is used as a pejorative word.[143] To describe judges as activist in this sense is to argue that they decide cases on the basis on their policy preferences rather than a faithful interpretation of the law.[144] When we generally speak of judicial activism in the United States, we generally imply the political rhetoric sense of the term. It is undeniable that some cases such as *Gibbons v. Ogden* (1824), *Brown v. Board of Education* (1954), *Gideon v. Wainwright* (1963) or *Miranda v. Arizona* (1966); are prime examples where the judicial branch has categorically and impartially revamped the system in order to uphold constitutional

---

[142] Ibid.
[143] Ibid.
[144] Ibid.

principles. On the other hand, there are some cases in which the Supreme Court of the United States has thoroughly legislated from the Bench. *Roe v. Wade* (1973) is probably the most eminent legal precedent ever legislated from the Bench in American legal history. The reason why *Roe* is believed to be legislated was because; although the Burger Court, which was a conservative bench, decided to nationally legalize abortion on the premise that a woman's right to have an abortion fell within the right to privacy, which is protected by the Fourteenth Amendment. The matter of abortion should have been left to state's authority to decide on whether abortion is legal or not. It was an infringement of the federal government onto state sovereignty. The legalization of abortion was an issue that became recurrent in mainstream culture during the late 1960s and early 1970s. The feminist movement has culturally gained ground and was politically determined to impact the system. And legalizing abortion was the main way to proceed to that end before the Equal Rights Amendment (ERA) could be brought again to the bargaining table. Despite the fact that the judges who decided in favor of legalizing abortion were conservatives; it is nonetheless undeniable that a strong political and public pressure was exerted over the Court. Abortion has become legal in the United States by unilateral implementation rather than by legislative or popular procedure. Since federal law overrides state law, the Supreme Court deciding on the issue strikingly undermines the authority and the sovereignty of state governments. States, perhaps in accordance or against their will; are compelled to uphold *Roe* has the law of the land. Again, the issue here is not about whether abortion is a crime or not. It is about the fact that the American people were left out of the political process regarding the legalization of abortion.

Judicial activism is an element, certainly pernicious, but central in the approach to judicial decisions because judges who have liberal and progressive tendencies, utilize the evolutionary theory[145] of the Constitution to precisely legislate a policy that could have not been invigorated by Congress with a left-leaning majority. This critic does not exempt right-leaning judges who also use judicial activism to enhance their own agenda when it fits them.

---

[145] The Evolutionary Theory of the Constitution suggests that the U.S. Constitution is a living document. Proponents of that theory argue that the U.S. Constitution shall be interpreted according to present times and present circumstances. The premise of their philosophy is based on the fact that the intention of the Framers of the Constitution is not necessarily adaptable to the realities of today.

Either way, judicial activism is merely an impediment to society when our legal philosophers, those who are supposed to uphold the integrity of the law, are mainly stimulated by political expediency. *Roe v. Wade* is not the only example of judicial activism. The case *Obergefell v. Hodges* (2015) is also an illustration of judicial activism. We all know that *Obergefell* is the famous case that legalize same-sex marriage. The problem with that case is not the mere fact that same-sex marriage is necessarily a spiteful thing. Far from that. Two individuals of the same sex who genuinely love each other, have the right to get married so long as their right to get married does not infringe the religious belief and freedom of others. The problem with *Obergefell* was the intent with which the case was decided. Under the constitutional model, which the American

Framers created, the role of judges is to apply the law but not to make the law; they are appointed to administer justice according to the law and not to change it or undermine it.[146] In *Obergefell,* the exact opposite of this principle was enacted. After the case was decided, and the Court's majority has agreed to legalize same-sex marriage from the Bench, Chief Justice John Roberts said in his dissenting argument:

"Today's decision rests on nothing more than the majority's own conviction that same-sex couples should be allowed to marry because they want to…Whatever force that belief may have as a matter of moral philosophy, it is no

---

[146] Zimmerman, Augusto, *Judicial Activism and Arbitrary Control: A Critical Analysis of Obergefell v. Hodges 566 US (2015)–The US Supreme Court Same-Sex Marriage.* 17 U. Notre Dame Austl. L. Rev. 77 (2015). HeinOnline. Article.

more basis in the Constitution than did the naked policy preferences."[147]

Obergefell has no substantive constitutional grounds. Nothing in the Constitution requires the redefinition of marriage in all 50 states, and five unelected justices do not have the authority to redefine marriage everywhere.[148] Again, the Court's decision to legalize same-sex marriage on constitutional ground is unwarranted because it, once again, encroached and violated state sovereignty like *Roe* did. Like *Roe, Obergefell* was decided on the premise of judicial activism because the legalization of same-sex marriage was becoming a political pressure that the federal government was compelled to pronounce itself upon it. Even President Obama was initially

---

[147] Ryan T. Anderson, Ph.D., *Judicial Activism on marriage Isn't the end—Here's what to do now.* Heritage Foundation. (2015). Article. Web.

[148] Ibid.

not in favor of same-sex marriage but evidently changed his mind for political reasons. Like in *Roe,* *Obergefell* undermines popular sovereignty. Nine unelected judges arbitrarily imposed upon the nation, a new concept of marriage that everyone must abide by otherwise, those who refuse to obey the Court's decision to legalize same-sex marriage will face the consequences of their disobedience. This is clearly a totalitarian method that was utilized to make a political opinion becoming a law. The legalization of same-sex marriage, like the legalization of abortion, did not undergo the legislative process nor through popular referendum. The American people were not directly consulted upon the issue. The federal government did not give the opportunity to the American people to decide upon the issue. Now we all have to abide by this decision arbitrarily made by the central authority.

Judicial activism is something that the American people shall and must pay more attention to. The Supreme Court detains the power to make laws, and to create constitutional rights that did previously not exist. We shall remember that the Supreme Court is a branch of the federal government. Its role has never been to legislate but solely to interpret the law according to the constitutional texts. The Supreme Court is a passive branch because the judges of the Court are not in the public eye. But in their black robes with their gavels, they have the authority to decide what case shall become the law of the land; therefore, a legal precedent. Through the Supreme Court, and especially through judicial activism, the federal government subtly but considerably expands its power over the people. It is gradually but surely becoming a totalitarian government that uses the law and its power to strengthen its authority. Like the other two branches of government, the Supreme Court of the United States substantively grew beyond its constitutional prerogatives. Who would have thought that the Supreme Court of the United States would be part of the aggrandizement of the federal government? The branch that was supposed to check the other two branches from expanding their power.

As I foresaid, the federal government is not only made up of the legislative branch and the executive branch. Yes, these two branches are very much prominent because one makes the law and the other enforces it; but the judiciary does not limit itself to solely interpret the law anymore. It also legislates the law whether it is voluntary or involuntary activism. For judges to legislate from the Bench is a constitutional coup d'état.

10.

The Market Is Better
Than Central-Planning

The United States is not a centrally-planned economy. It is way far from it. It is also no longer a laissez-faire economy like it used to be before the Great Depression. Like most Western countries, we have a regulated market economy properly known as a mixed economy. We have a market economy in which the federal government plays a substantial role in economic activities. Consequently, we do have a planned economy because the market is regulated. Our economic system is a mixed economy in which we, now, have a mixture of capitalist elements such as access to private property, private businesses, and entrepreneurship; and socialist elements such as the welfare state, state-owned enterprises, a partially publicly-subsidized healthcare, government-owned schools and public housing. The United States is definitely a planned and regulated market economy

Before the 1930s, we, in the United States, had a laissez-faire economy. The federal government was remarkably minimal to quasi non-existent in economic activities. In 1913, just prior to World War I, federal government expenditures were 2.5 of Gross National Product and by 1990 they had risen to 22.5 percent of GNP.[149] Before the Great Depression, the United States experienced extraordinary economic prosperity. Regulations on taxes were

---

[149] Holcombe, Randall, *The Growth of the Federal Government in the 1920s, Cato Journals.* Cato Institute. Vol. 16, No. 2 (1996). Article.

extensively minimal, the conditions to open a business were strikingly loose with very excessively few restrictions. Almost no licenses required to maintain the management of an enterprise. Individuals were free from government control over their economic activities. Laissez-faire works best for economic growth because it provides individuals with the greatest incentive to create wealth.[150] The claim that a laissez-faire economy impoverished the worker could not be more misleading. Factory owners did not have the power to force workers to labor in their factories; all they could do was offering work at a given wage to people who were free to accept the offer or to reject it and seek for work

---

[150] Reed, Lawrence W. *Laissez-Faire and Economic Growth.* Mackinac Center For Public Policy. (2001). Article. Web.

elsewhere.[151] In the nineteenth century, the level of productivity in the United States was essentially high. In 1870, according to a research conducted by Michael Cox and Richard Alm; the average worker worked 3,069 hours a year.[152] As his productivity increased, by 1913, he could enjoy a much-improved standard of living working only 2,632 hours.[153] The 1920s was an overall period of vast economic expansion with few intrinsic recessions. And laissez-faire economy made that expansion possible. Ownership of cars, new household appliances, and housing were spread widely through the population.[154] New products and

---

[151] Yaron Brook and Don Watkins, *Capitalism In No Way Created Poverty, It Inherited It.* Forbes. (2013). Article. Web.

[152] Ibid.
[153] Ibid.
[154] Smiley, Gene, *The U.S. Economy in the 1920s.* EH.net. Economic History Association.

processes of producing those products drove this growth.[155] The combination of the widening use of electricity in production and the growing adoption of the moving assembly line in manufacturing combined to bring on a continuing rise in the productivity of labor and capital.[156] According to Dr. Milton Friedman, the quintessential reason for the economic growth of the 1920s was the stability of prices through the monetary policy of the Federal Reserve from 1923 to 1928.[157] The labor force also grew. For skilled and semi-skilled male workers, real average weekly earnings rose 5.3 percent between 1923 and 1929,[158] while real average

---

[155] Ibid.

[156] Ibid.

[157] *The Economy's New Clothes: Milton Friedman on the New Economy.* Uncommon Knowledge. Peter Robinson interviewing Milton Friedman in 2000. Hoover Institution Production. Interview Video

[158] Smiley, Gene, *The U.S. Economy in the 1920s.* EH.net. Economic History Association.

weekly earnings for unskilled males rose 8.7 percent during 1923 and 1929.[159] Real weekly earnings for females rose on 1.7 percent between 1923 and 1929.[160] Let's remind ourselves that during that period, the federal government play a very restricted role within economic mechanisms. The people were free to invest wherever they see fit in order to generate profit. The data demonstrated that the living standard of the average American was relatively high due to a deregulated market.

The Great Depression, however, happened at the end of the 1920s. It was the greatest economic downturn in modern history. Its consequences have destroyed the lives of millions of Americans. Its impact was so

---

[159] Ibid.
[160] Ibid.

prodigiously devastating that it has annihilated Europe and some advanced economies in Asia.

The mainstream narrative regarding the main cause of the Great Depression was attributed to a failure of laissez-faire economics. Left-leaning intellectuals have argued that the crash of the stock market of 1929 was due to an unregulated economy that, did not only create a tremendous gap in income inequality between rich and poor, but also incentivized a distortion of the business cycle. This argument has regrettably become the myth that is now conveyed in the American collective consciousness and in the American educational system. To simplify concisely the argument that left-wing intellectuals maintained on this specific subject, the Great Depression would have not occurred if the federal government had regulated the economy beforehand. The truth is that the Great Depression was not created by the failure of the free-market. It was the government that has unintentionally generated the Great Depression through a failure of monetary policy implemented by the Federal Reserve between 1928 and 1929 then through the interventionist policies of Herbert Hoover in the early days of the Depression.

The failure of this monetary policy has given to the federal government the opportunity to not only intervene in the economy but also to expand its power beyond its constitutional prerogatives. What created the Great Depression was a failure of the Real Bills Doctrine.[161] The Federal Reserve contracted the money supply to commercial banks at higher

---

[161] The Real Bills Doctrine is a monetary policy in which currency is issued in exchange at a discount for short-term debt. It is the transaction between a bank and a business that results in the issuance of money into the economy. It was the monetary policy of the Federal Reserve during the 1920s.

rates, so individuals and private businesses could not easily borrow and spend on whatever goods and services they would like. This contraction of money supply to commercial banks dropped the inflation rate to one-third of the nominal rate and subsequently deflated price stability. This deflation accelerated the crash because the economy was expanding too rapidly than the long trend established by the authorities of the Federal Reserve. The first signs of serious trouble appeared in 1929, the concerns of Federal Reserve Bank centered on the quality of bank loans.[162] The supply of credit included far too many speculative loans based on stock shares, real estate loans, and government securities.[163] In his 860-page book

---

[162] Timberlake, Richard H. "Gold Standards and the Real Bills Doctrine in U.S. Monetary Policy," *Econ Journal Watch*. Volume 2, Number 2, (2005), pp 196-233. Article. P.215.

[163] Ibid.

entitled *A Monetary History of The United States* (1963); Dr. Friedman argued that the Federal Reserve misused the Real Bills Doctrine in attempting to control stock market prices although its mission was to strictly keep general prices stable; not the ones of the stock market. The Fed's intent to dictate the price of the stock market generated the crash. The Great Depression was a uniquely severe contraction—real Gross Domestic Product (GDP) fell for four years before finally beginning to recover.[164] The unemployment rate stayed persistently high at more than 14 percent for ten years (1931 to 1940).[165] By contrast, the economy recovered rapidly after a sharp contraction in 1921.[166] Real

---

[164] Edwards, Chris, "The Government and the Great Depression," *Tax &Budget Bulletin*, Cato Institute. (2005). Article. Web.

[165] Ibid.
[166] Ibid.

output fell 9 percent in 1921 and unemployment rose to 11.7 percent.[167] But the economy bounced back with output recovering all its lost ground in 1922.[168] Unemployment fell to 6.7 percent in 1922 and 2.4 percent in 1923.[169] The secret to this rapid economic recovery was that the federal government generally stood aside and let the market recover by itself—wages and prices adjusted, resources shifted to new areas of growth, profits recovered, business optimism returned, and investment rose.[170] In contradistinction to the rapid recovery of the economy through self-regulation in the early 1920s, government policies in the 1930s prevented the U.S. economy from recovering as fast as it should be.[171] Of course, this lengthy but

---

[167] Ibid.
[168] Ibid.
[169] Ibid.
[170] Ibid.
[171] Ibid.

truthfully necessary explanation about what caused the Great Depression will never be shared in the mainstream culture because it will distort the fallacious narrative that has been tacitly constructed by the left intelligentsia over the years. The left intelligentsia has successfully ingrained into the collective consciousness of the American people, the resentment against laissez-faire that we are witnessing today. This resentment against laissez-faire economics is now spread in history books through high schools, universities, and in the mainstream media. Unless the average American citizen seeks to advance his own knowledge regarding the origins of the Great Depression and why we have an economically totalitarian government; he should surely not expect to learn or gain that knowledge from the mainstream media or universities.

It is interesting to see that the federal government which was, certainly yet involuntarily, the instigator of the Great Depression; is that same government that claims to have the solution to solve the crisis. The economic policies of the New Deal were merely fiscal stimuli programs that slowed the economic recovery because the government dictated prices as well as it detained an extended authority over the means of production. Government intervention in the economy simply delayed the natural progression that was supposed to take place through self-regulatory mechanisms. Increasing government spending and reducing government taxes simply reduces the purchasing power of the consumer and also increases unemployment because this mechanism upsurges inflation. That is why it took such a long time for unemployment rate to shrink to an acceptable rate. Before the Great Depression, the American people viewed the federal government as a necessary evil; a government that was created to fulfill its minarchist role, which was to leave the citizens alone to pursue their self-interests but to protect their rights and to defend the national interest. The outcome of the Great Depression falsely changed that perception of the American people toward government. According to a 2002 poll; old yet relevant, which was conducted by Gallup; found that 46 percent of the American people believe that most money in an economic stimulus bill should be used for increasing government spending.[172] According to a 2015 poll conducted by Pew Research Center, 55 percent of the American people believe that the

---

[172] Jones, Jeffrey M. *Public Divided on How Best to Stimulate Economy.* Gallup. (2002). Article. Web.

federal government should play a major role in the economy.[173] According to a 2019 recent poll by *ISideWith;* 71 percent of the American people believe that the federal government should use economic stimulus to aid the country during times of recession[174] similar to what President Roosevelt did in the 1930s and early 1940s. These results substantiated a progressive trust in government power over the last two decades. The majority of the American people grew up to believe and accept that the federal government is the cure to societal upheavals. The myth of the federal government as the benefactor of society is certainly implanted in American society but it is not yet absolute.

---

[173] *Role of Government, Free Market Economy, and Attitudes Toward Public Spending and Taxation.* The Opportunity Agenda. (2019). Article. Web.

[174] Polls. I Side With⋯.

Today, the American economy is a market economy that is more than ever regulated by the federal government. The federal government has never succeeded in implementing an economic policy that delivered long-term benefits to society as a whole. But it did successfully manage to impose its legal totalitarian power over the American power through an effectuation of relentless regulations. Bureaucracy is now ubiquitous and omnipotent at all levels of society, whether it is on the political, economic and social aspect. The federal government now controls the price of goods and services through regulations and licenses. Friedrich August von Hayek published in 1944 *The Road to Serfdom* in which he warned Western societies about the danger of central planning. He argued that the government is inclined to intrinsically mismanage resources because it will spend more money and create less value. Government spends money that is not its own on someone else. Moreover, the retention of the means of production by a government inevitably leads to central planning then to totalitarianism. This frightful prophecy from one of the greatest economists and political philosophers in modern history, was not unsubstantiated. The federal government has ruined the sectors in which it has intervened. The same has happened in the United Kingdom right after World War II, when the Labour Party instigated a socialist agenda to rule the kingdom. It nationalized major industries such as healthcare, education, housing, energy, and manufacturing businesses. The whole British economy in the 1950s and 1960s was relatively stagnated. The post-war economy tumbled into the public sector, where they were subject to elaborate planning controls.[175] The Labour Party created a gigantic welfare state akin the United States during the FDR era. Economic growth was slow, and the national output decreased due to a lack of innovation within industries controlled by the British government. Central planning is not a myth. It is real and it is a danger. It has destroyed every government and society that have tried it. The Soviet Union, Cuba, and Eastern European countries are prime examples of the failure of central planning. The federal government of the United States has an excessive authority over the economy of the country. It is a danger to our freedom because the bureaucrats in Washington are taking the people on the verge of a centrally-planned economy. It is imperative for the federal

---

[175] Brown, Derek, *1945-51: Labour and the creation of the welfare state.* The Guardian. (2001). Article. Web.

government to withdraw from economic activities and to let the people pursuing their own self-interests. It has been numerously proven that an economy grows faster and recovers quicker when the individuals are free from government control.

References

1. Editors, "BRIA 14 3 How Welfare Began in the United States," *Bill of Rights in Action,* Constitutional Rights Foundation. (1998). Article.

2. Ibid.

3. Ibid.

4. Ibid.

5. Ibid.

6. Ibid.

7. Ibid.

8. Ibid.

9. Ibid.

10. Powell, Jim, *How FDR's New Deal Harmed Millions of Poor People.* Cato Institute. (2003). Article. Web.

11. Ibid.

12. Ibid.

13. Ibid.

14. Ibid.

15. Ibid.

16. Ibid.

17. Daniel, *Why Did The New Deal Fail?* Medium.com. (2016). Article. Web.

18. Ibid.

19. Ibid.

20. Rector, Robert, *The War on Poverty: 50 years of Failure.* The Heritage Foundation. (2014). Article. Web.

21. Ibid.

22. Ibid.

23. Ibid.

24. Ibid.

25. Ibid.

26. Ferrera, Peter, *'Welfare State' Doesn't Adequately Describe How Much America's Poor Control Your Wallet.* Forbes. (2013). Article. Web.

27. Ibid.

28. *Inflation and CPI Consumer Index 1940-1949,* InflationData.com. (2019). Index Charts.

29. McMorris, Bill, *Wage Hikes Depressed Low-Skilled Unemployment.* The Washington Free Beacon. (2016). Article. Web.

30. Ibid.

31. Clemens, Jefferey, *The Minimum Wage and The Great Recession: Evidence from The Current Population Survey.* National Bureau of Economic Research. (2015). Article.

32.Millsap, Adam, *How Higher Minimum Wages Impact Employment,* Forbes. (2018). Article. Web.

33.Dara Lee Luca and Michael Luca, *Survival of the Fittest: The Impact of the minimum Wage on Firm Exit.* Harvard Business School, Mathematica Policy Research. (2017-2018). Working Paper 17-088. Article.

34.Gehr, Jessica, "Doubling Down: How Work Requirements in Public Benefit Programs Hurt Low-Wage Workers." *Policy Brief.* CLASP: Policy solutions that work for low-income people. (2017). Article.

35.Ibid.

36.Jasay, Anthony, "Paternalism and Employment," *Political Economy Concisely: Essays On Policy That Do Not Work and Markets That Do.* (2009). P .182. ISBN: 978-0-86597-778-5. Print.

37. Jasay, Anthony, *The Vicious Circle of Social Kindness,* Financial Times, (1994). Columns

38. Ibid.

39. Ibid.

40. Ibid.

41. Jasay, Anthony, "Paternalism and Employment," *Political Economy Concisely: Essays On Policy That Do Not Work and Markets That Do.* (2009). p.183. ISBN: 978-0-86597-778-5. Print.

42. Ibid. p. 201.

43. Letitia Stein, Susan Cornwell, Joseph Tanfani, *Inside the Progressive Movement Roiling the Democratic Party.* Reuters. (2018). Article. Web.

44. Associate Press. *Obamacare's Fines Are Not The Big Stick Everybody Thought,* ModernHealthcare.com (2018). Article. Web.

45. *What Is the Individual Mandate for Health Care Reform?* TurboTax. Updated in 2018. Article. Web.

46. Ibid.

47. Editorials, *Obamacare Failure: Uninsured Rate Hasn't Budged In 3 years, CDC Says.* Investor's Business Daily. (2018). Article. Web.

48. Ibid.

49. Ibid.

50. Hawkins, Marcus, *10 Reasons Obamacare Is a Failure,* ThoughtCo. (2017). Article. Web.

51. Feldpausch, Sarah, *Six Years on Obamacare Has Failed to Deliver,* Americans for Tax Reform, (2016). Article. Web.

52. Ibid.

53. Baum, Caroline, *Why Healthcare Is Not A Right.* Economics21. (2015). Article. Web.

54. Ibid.

55. Ibid.

56. Editors, *Swedes face problems with healthcare system.* The Business Times. (2018). Article. Web.

57. Ibid.

58. Ibid.

59. Bernpaintner, Klaus, *The Truth About SwedenCare,* Mises Institute, (2013). Article. Web.

60. Ibid.

61. Ibid.

62. Hogberg, David, *Sweden's Single-Payer Health System Provides A Warning to Other Nations.* National Center for Public Policy Research. (2007). Article.

63. Amadeo, Kimberly, *Progressive Taxes With Examples: How a Progressive Tax System Helps the Economy.* The Balance. (2019). Article. Web.

64. "Theme 3: Fairness in Taxes: Lesson 3: Progressive Taxes", *Understanding Taxes.* Internal Revenue Service. Article.

65. McDaniel, Mario, *The Disadvantages of Progressive Taxes.* Pocket Sense. (2017). Article. Web.

66. Ibid.

67. Wolfe, Michelle, *Advantages and Disadvantages of Progressive Tax.* Sapling. (2011). Article. Web.

68. Ibid.

69. Staff, "Key Elements of the U.S. Tax System." *Tax Policy Center Briefing Book.* Tax Policy Center. (2018). Article.

70. Cohen, Patricia, *Study Finds Local Taxes Hit Lower Wage Earners Harder,* The New York Times. (2015). Article. Web.

71. Ayres, Crystal, *11 Biggest Progressive Tax Pros and Cons.* Vittana Personal Finance Blog. Article. Web.

72. Ibid.

73. Sowell, Thomas, *The Many Benefits of a Flat Tax.* St. Louis Post-Dispatch. (1996).

74. Ibid.

75. Ibid.

76. "The Constitution of the United States," Amendment 1.

77. "U.S. Institutions-Why is the First Amendment Important?" *Ideals and Institutions.* Editorials. (2017). Article. Web.

78. Ibid.

79. Ibid.

80. Representative James P. McGovern and Senator Marco Rubio, "Freedom of Expression in China: A Privilege, Not a

Right." *Congressional-Executive Commission on China*. Article.

81. Ibid.

82. Ibid.

83. "Politically Correct" *Merriam-Webster*.

84. Wagoner, Josh, *How Political Correctness and Identity Politics Are Destroying America*. The Daily Caller. (2018). Article. Web.

85. Ibid.

86. Ibid.

87. Ibid.

88. Codevilla, Angelo, *The Rise of Political Correctness,* Independent Institute. (2016). Article. Web.

89. McCullough, J.J. *How Canada Bans Books*. National Review. (2018).. Article. Web.

90. Ibid.

91. Ibid.

92. Ibid.

93. Kenton, Will, *Fiscal Policy,* Investopedia, Updated in May 2019.

94. Blinder, Alan S. *Keynesian Economics.* The Library of Economics and Liberty. Article. Web.

95. Weil, David, N. *Fiscal Policy.* The Library of Economics and Liberty. Article.

96. Ibid.

97. Ibid.

98. Amadeo, Kimberly, *Contractionary Fiscal Policy and Its Purpose With Examples.* The Balance. (2019). Article. Web.

99. Poverty Thresholds for 2018. Data.

100. Ibid.

101. Pettinger, Tejvan, *Monetary Policy vs Fiscal Policy.* Economics Help. (2018). Article. Web.

102. Ibid.

103. Blanchard, Olivier, "2. Monetary policy affects both the actual and the natural rate of unemployment." *Monetary Policy and Unemployment.* (2003). Article.

104. Mester, Loretta J., *Five Points About Monetary Policy and Financial Stability.* The Federal Reserve Bank of Cleveland. (2016). Article.

105. Pettinger, Tejvan, *Monetary policy vs. Fiscal Policy.* Economic Help. (2018). Article. Web.

106. Ibid.

107. Sowell, Thomas, "Social Factors," *Wealth, Poverty and Politics.* Basic Books. (2016). ISBN: 978-0-465-09676-3. P. 164. Print.

108. Ibid. p. 164.

109. Ibid. p. 164.

110. "Population" Ibid. p. 181.

111. "Population" Ibid. p. 181.

112. Courtney, Jennifer, *Problems with Common Core that Need Attention,* Classical Conversations. Classical Christian Community. (2019). Article. Web.

113. Ibid.

114. Ibid.

115. Ibid.

116. Pullman, Joy, *How Common Core Damages Student's College Readiness.* The James G. Martin Center For Academic Renewal. (2017). Article. Web.

117. Ibid.

118. Ibid.

119. SAT Score Data. (2017).

120. Mosteller, Jeremiah, *The Militarization of Police*. Charles Koch Institute. Article. Web.

121. Ibid.

122. Ibid.

123. Ibid.

124. Ibid.

125. Ibid.

126. Ibid.

127. Ibid.

128. Ibid.

129. Akpan, Nsikan, *Police Militarization Fails to Protect Officers and Targets Black Communities, Study Finds.* (2018). Article. Web.

130. Mummolo, Jonathan, *Militarization Fails to Enhance Police Safety or Reduce Crime but may Harm Police Reputation.* Proceedings of the National Academy of

Sciences of the United States of America. (2018). Article.

131. Ibid.

132. Ibid.

133. Jefferey T. Fowler, Ph.D., *Police Militarization in America—A Negative or Positive Trend?* In Homeland Security. (2017). Article. Web.

134. Ibid.

135. Ibid.

136. Lawson Jr., Edward. *Evidence Suggests The Militarization of Police Forces Leads To More Civilian Deaths.* LSE US Centre. (2018). Article. Web.

137. Ibid.

138. Ibid.

139. Ferrera, Victoria, *Police Militarization in America: The Land of the Free and the Home*

of Contradictions. Ramapo College of New Jersey. (2017). Article.

140. Tate, Neal, "Judicial Review," *Law,* Encyclopedia Britannica.

141. Roosevelt, Kermit, "Judicial Activism," *Law,* Encyclopedia Britannica.

142. Ibid.

143. Ibid.

144. Ibid.

145. The Evolutionary Theory of the Constitution suggests that the U.S. Constitution is a living document. Proponents of that theory argue that the U.S. Constitution shall be interpreted according to present times and present circumstances. The premise of their philosophy is based on the fact that the intention of the Framers of the Constitution is not necessarily adaptable to the realities of today.

146. Zimmerman, Augusto, *Judicial Activism and Arbitrary Control: A Critical Analysis of Obergefell v. Hodges 566 US (2015)-The US Supreme Court Same-Sex Marriage.* 17 U. Notre Dame Austl. L. Rev. 77 (2015). HeinOnline. Article.

147. Ryan T. Anderson, Ph.D., *Judicial Activism on marriage Isn't the end—Here's what to do now.* Heritage Foundation. (2015). Article. Web.

148. Ibid.

149. Holcombe, Randall, *The Growth of the Federal Government in the 1920s, Cato Journals.* Cato Institute. Vol. 16, No. 2 (1996). Article.

150. Reed, Lawrence W. *Laissez-Faire and Economic Growth.* Mackinac Center For Public Policy. (2001). Article. Web.

151. Yaron Brook and Don Watkins, *Capitalism In No Way Created Poverty, It Inherited It.* Forbes. (2013). Article. Web.

152. Ibid.

153. Ibid.

154. Smiley, Gene, *The U.S. Economy in the 1920s.* EH.net. Economic History Association.

155. Ibid.

156. Ibid.

157. *The Economy's New Clothes: Milton Friedman on the New Economy.* Uncommon Knowledge. Peter Robinson interviewing Milton Friedman in 2000. Hoover Institution Production. Interview Video

158. Smiley, Gene, *The U.S. Economy in the 1920s.* EH.net. Economic History Association.

159. Ibid.

160.   Ibid.

161.   The Real Bills Doctrine is a monetary policy in which currency is issued in exchange at a discount for short-term debt. It is the transaction between a bank and a business that results in the issuance of money into the economy. It was the monetary policy of the Federal Reserve during the 1920s.

162.   Timberlake, Richard H. "Gold Standards and the Real Bills Doctrine in U.S. Monetary Policy," *Econ Journal Watch.* Volume 2, Number 2, (2005), pp 196-233. Article. P.215.

163.   Ibid.

164.   Edwards, Chris, "The Government and the Great Depression," *Tax &Budget Bulletin*, Cato Institute. (2005). Article. Web.

165.   Ibid.

166.   Ibid.

167.   Ibid.

168. Ibid.

169. Ibid.

170. Ibid.

171. Ibid.

172. Jones, Jeffrey M. *Public Divided on How Best to Stimulate Economy.* Gallup. (2002). Article. Web.

173. *Role of Government, Free Market Economy, and Attitudes Toward Public Spending and Taxation.* The Opportunity Agenda. (2019). Article. Web.

174. Polls. I Side With⋯.

175. Brown, Derek, *1945-51: Labour and the creation of the welfare state.* The Guardian. (2001). Article. Web.

www.ingramcontent.com/pod-product-compliance
Lightning Source LLC
Chambersburg PA
CBHW060457290526
45791CB00001B/153